Aimless in Banaras

Bishwanath Ghosh, born in Kanpur on 26 December 1970, is the author of the hugely popular *Chai, Chai: Travels in Places Where You Stop But Never Get Off.* He's also a Hindi poet, who has two well-received compilations—*Jiyo Banaras* and *Tedhi-Medhi Lakeeren*—to his credit. His other books include *Tamarind City: Where Modern India Began*; *Longing, Belonging: An Outsider at Home in Calcutta*; and *Gazing at Neighbours: Travels Along the Line that Partitioned India*. He is an Associate Editor with *The Hindu* newspaper and lives in Calcutta.

ALSO BY BISHWANATH GHOSH

Chai, Chai: Travels in Places Where You Stop but Never Get Off (2009)

Tamarind City: Where Modern India Began (2012)

Longing, Belonging: An Outsider at Home in Calcutta (2014)

Gazing at Neighbours: Travels Along the Lines That Partitioned India (2017)

BISHWANATH GHOSH

Aimless in Banaras

WANDERINGS IN
INDIA'S HOLIEST CITY

First published by Tranquebar, an imprint of Westland Publications Private Limited, in 2019

Published by Tranquebar, an imprint of Westland Books, a division of Nasadiya Technologies Private Limited, in 2024

No. 269/2B, First Floor, 'Irai Arul', Vimalraj Street, Nethaji Nagar, Alapakkam Main Road, Maduravoyal, Chennai 600095

Westland, the Westland logo, Tranquebar and the Tranquebar logo are the trademarks of Nasadiya Technologies Private Limited, or its affiliates.

Copyright © Bishwanath Ghosh, 2019

Bishwanath Ghosh asserts the moral right to be identified as the author of this work.

ISBN: 9789360456078

10 9 8 7 6 5 4 3 2 1

The views and opinions expressed in this work are the author's own and the facts are as reported by him, and the publisher is in no way liable for the same.

All rights reserved

Typeset by SÜRYA, New Delhi

Printed at Nutech Print Services, India

No part of this book may be reproduced, or stored in a retrieval system, or transmitted in any form or by any means, electronic, mechanical, photocopying, recording, or otherwise, without express written permission of the publisher.

For
मॉं जी

Author's Note

THE CITY DESCRIBED in this book is known variously as Kashi, Banaras, Benares and Varanasi. I have chosen to call it Banaras because I find it most evocative of the culture it cradles and also because the name, when suffixed with an 'i', denotes its most important element: its people.

Quintessential Banarasis inhabit its ghats and galis, and those are the places where this book is set. The Banaras that thrives outside the mindboggling maze of ghats and galis is hardly different from the other cities dotting the map of Uttar Pradesh and is of no interest to me.

Prologue: Banaras Beckons

A DOZEN PYRES burned at the Manikarnika Ghat that afternoon. Under the dark August clouds, the flames looked their colourful best: violent yellows and volatile oranges dancing on mortal remains. The Ganga, swollen and muddied by the monsoon, watched the spectacle with a mix of indulgence and indifference. She would carry away the ashes once the flames died.

Manikarnika Ghat, dating back to the time when gods and goddesses still walked the earth, makes Banaras the most favoured destination for the dead. Devout Hindus believe that if you are cremated at Manikarnika, you go straight to heaven, with no stopovers in the form of rebirths.

One of the pyres burning was that of my mother. She had not come to Banaras to die, unlike many others who do once they realise their end is near. She was only fifty-nine. She did have a heart condition that was slowly deteriorating, but death was the last thing on her mind when she and my father had set out from Kanpur, about 350 kilometres away, to visit my younger brother who was posted in Banaras. One afternoon, as the three of them were having lunch, she suddenly arched back and died. When the news travelled 2,000 kilometres south to reach me in Chennai, it suddenly struck me that Banaras had been thrust on me.

Thirty-nine years before, when I was still in my mother's womb, my maternal grandfather happened to visit Banaras. While praying at the Vishwanath Temple there, he decided that if his daughter gave birth to a boy, the child would be named after the presiding deity: Vishwanath, the Lord of the Universe, another name for Lord Shiva, spelt by Bengalis as Bishwanath.

And now I was to rush to the very place where my name had been decided when I was still in the womb, to cremate the owner of that womb. The distance of 2,000 kilometres needed to be covered as soon as possible.

I took the first available flight to Delhi and from there, the next morning, flew to Banaras. I was surprisingly calm when I saw my mother on a bed of ice. My body continued to have its natural cravings, such as the urge to smoke.

Since my brother had moved to Banaras only recently, he hardly had a circle of friends. Barely seven or eight people, nearly all of them his colleagues and acquaintances, were in attendance when I arrived. That was how big the funeral procession was going to be.

One of them, an influential journalist, had arranged for the cremation at Manikarnika. I asked him if the ghat had an electric crematorium. He said Manikarnika did not have one, but Harishchandra Ghat did. I suggested that we go to Harishchandra Ghat instead, because I did not want to watch my mother slowly melting into ashes on a pyre.

A small argument broke out. The majority opinion was that only the fortunate get to be cremated at Manikarnika and that I would be committing a grave sin by denying my mother her ticket to heaven. I looked at my father. He did not oppose me, but I could sense he was on their side.

The body was placed on a string cot and we set out for Manikarnika on a mini-truck. The truck dropped us at the mouth of an alley, and from there we had to walk up to the ghat, the cot carried on four shoulders. My brother and I refused to let go of the weight, while others took turns in lending their shoulders.

One alley led to another. So narrow were they that my free shoulder often brushed past sachets of shampoo and paan masala dangling in shops. At one point I stepped on a cavity in the brick path and twisted my ankle. But I walked on despite the sharp pain because my feet had to be in tandem with the three other pairs walking with the cot.

The overcast sky finally came into view and so did the river. We had arrived at the kingdom of the dead, though at first glance it resembled a timber store: we were surrounded by logs of wood piled up high enough to reach the roof of a two-storey building.

Manikarnika Ghat is indeed a kingdom. Cremations are conducted exclusively by members of the doam caste, who are governed by the doam raja, or the king of doams. He is considered far more powerful than the king of Banaras—not without reason. The influence and fortunes of a political ruler invariably change with times, but the ruler of doams need not worry about the vicissitudes of life because death is certain.

An elderly Bengali priest met us at the ghat. He asked me to remove my clothes and handed me two white sheets to wear: one was to be tied around the waist and the other thrown over the shoulders. As I carried out his instructions, a friendly doam appeared and said the pyre was ready on the terrace of the ghat.

While the others carried the cot to the terrace, I stayed back with the priest for a certain ritual that I—as the elder son—was required to perform before lighting the pyre. The two of us sat on our haunches in a corner of the ghat where the priest made a paste by mashing rice grains, curd, milk, sweets and banana. He then asked me to draw lines on the floor with the paste. The lines I drew under his direction resembled a square puzzle. Were they meant to demystify life?

After the ritual I made my way to the terrace, where I found my mother's pyre placed on the far end. Reaching it was like walking through a furnace because bodies were already burning on the terrace. On seeing me, the doam handed me a flaming sheaf of grass and asked me to touch the fire to my mother's lips. Barely had I done that—her lips instantly blackened—when he took away the burning grass from my hand and placed it between the logs for them to catch fire.

'Please leave now, all of you,' he told us firmly, 'wait downstairs. I will call you when it is all done.'

So I had just performed something I always dreaded: mukhagni, touching the fire to the mouth of the dead before it is consigned to flames. Electric crematoriums automatically spare you this ritual, and even in traditional crematoriums in bigger cities, families can take liberties with the tradition. But this was Manikarnika, the mother of all cremation grounds, where tampering with tradition is not allowed.

I felt a sense of accomplishment as I walked through the furnace once again—now I had the courage to look at the other burning pyres—and climbed down the terrace.

I also felt free. The one question that had been nagging me for several years—what if Mother died?—was now out of the way. I finally began to take notice of Manikarnika. Twelve bodies were burning in all, six on the terrace and six on the steps leading to the river. More bodies were coming in. They would keep on coming. The fire never dies at Manikarnika, said to be even older than Banaras—and no one knows exactly how old Banaras is.

We found places to sit at the ghat and made ourselves comfortable. As chance would have it, the funeral procession of eight people included our long-time neighbour from Kanpur: he happened to be visiting his ancestral village near Banaras when he got the news and had come over right away. His presence at the ghat was comforting. It made us, especially my father, feel less unfamiliar with the surroundings.

One of my brother's acquaintances got tea for all of us, and soon we were chatting like friends who met every evening at the neighbourhood tea stall. Goats and cows looked for garlands and flowers to munch on. Dogs sniffed around nervously. Other mourners had also found their own corners. Death was a business here, not a tragedy. The loss of a loved one ceased to be a personal loss the moment you emerged from the narrow streets onto the ghat, where you found many other bodies awaiting cremation—and many others already burning.

From time to time, a speck of ash, originating from some pyre or other, would land on our tea. Those who noticed the ash on their tea drank it anyway. For the superstitious—and my mother was superstitious—drinking ash-laced tea would amount to drinking death, but the wise would see that as accepting death.

I felt like smoking and walked up to the tea stall to buy a cigarette. I stood on the steps, away from my father's view, and lit up. He knows I smoke but I do not smoke in front of him. I surveyed the river. I had known the Ganga all my life—I grew up by it, in Kanpur—but today, for the first time, I stood on its banks bound by duty.

I looked at the boats floating past. Their occupants looked at me curiously. Actually they were looking at the kingdom of death—the living museum that makes Banaras famous world over. I was merely one of the many displays. What they didn't realise was that I, too, like them, was a spectator. And unlike them, even though I was in mourners' robes, I was constantly taking mental notes, something I could use in a future book.

The thought of a few thousand people reading that book and sharing my sorrow had presently divided it into so many minute pieces that there was hardly any sorrow left for me to feel. Far from being a grieving son, I felt like a writer who had lucked into rich material.

The doam sent word that the cremation was over. It had taken nearly three hours. The priest asked me and my brother to accompany him to the terrace. The pyre, which had stood at about three feet until three hours ago, was now reduced to a bed of smouldering ashes.

The priest handed me a clay pitcher and asked me to fill it up with water from the river. When I returned with the filled pitcher, he asked me to empty it over the cinder. I heard a hissing sound as I poured the water and then nothing remained of my mother—even the smoulder in her ashes died. But something did remain: a tiny charred piece, which the doam handed us on a clay bowl.

'This is your mother's navel,' the priest explained. 'Fire burns the entire body into ashes, but the navel is indestructible. Now immerse it in the Ganga and with that we are done for the day.'

My brother and I walked down the steps of Manikarnika and together we flung the navel into the river and freed our mother from the cycle of birth and death.

My mother died in 2009. Six years later, I am back in Banaras. I have the contract for the book whose imaginary success had seen me through her cremation.

'Nothing is permanent,' the waiter is telling an Italian couple as I come to the terrace of the riverside lodge for breakfast. 'Everything must come to an end.' I have arrived late to catch the context, but I can see the couple listening to him wide-eyed.

'What is there today,' he continues, 'will not be there tomorrow. That is the truth.' The waiter is a boy, barely eighteen.

The people of Banaras—and I mean those living by the river—are one of the happiest people on earth. Unhurried and unworried, living and letting live, helping themselves to a small dose of bhang, or cannabis, every evening to celebrate the extension of their existence on this planet by one more day, they come across as sages who have answers to life's square puzzles.

After a few days in the city, it is not difficult to see why they are the way they are.

Banaras—Kashi during ancient times, Benares during the British rule, and now officially Varanasi—is essentially a string of eighty-plus ghats that emphasise the river's northward twist. The centrepiece of this string is the Dashashwamedha Ghat, occupied during the day by priests conducting business with pilgrims, boatmen calling out to tourists, and fake sadhus obliging photographers for a small fee, and during the night by locals who come in small groups to wind down after they have had their daily dose of bhang.

It's a happy ghat, where lamps are waved at the river—Goddess Ganga—shortly after sunset. But hardly fifteen ghats upstream is Harishchandra Ghat, and barely fifteen ghats downstream, Manikarnika. Since cremation at these two ghats is a public spectacle, it is almost impossible to miss the burning pyres. The images serve a daily reminder to the people of Banaras: no matter who you are, you will end up at either of these ghats someday.

So in Banaras, where thousands come each day to seek answers to life's square puzzles, you realise that life isn't a puzzle after all. It's pretty much a straight line, starting with birth and ending with death.

PART ONE

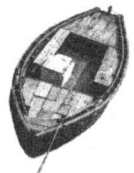

1.

AT TWO IN the morning, when Banaras takes a breather, I present myself at the Vishwanath Temple to find some hundred people already in the queue.

In an hour from now, the Lord of the Universe will be roused and bathed and decorated for the first worship of the day, the Mangala aarti. The earlier you arrive the closer you are placed to the sanctum sanctorum when priests conduct this elaborate ritual. Even a small delay in joining the queue can squander the chances of an unhindered view.

This is a ticketed event for which only about 400 people are allowed in. Devotees come from far and near—mostly far. An elderly Tamil man walking past the queue enquires aloud: 'Is this the way to the Mangala aarti?'

'Yes, but please join the queue,' someone replies.

'But I have a ticket,' the man waves a paper.

'We all have tickets.'

'But I have a 300-rupee ticket.'

'We all have 300-rupee tickets.'

The disappointed man retraces his steps and disappears towards the end of the line. More such ignorant souls are humbled in turn.

Chatter fills up the alley containing the queue. My ears can tell that Tamils, Telugus and Bengalis—in that order—outnumber the others. The voices, irrespective of the language, betray impatience: killing time is not easy when not in possession of a mobile phone, which is prohibited inside the temple and must be deposited in a locker at one of the flower shops.

A small group of Tamils right behind me in the queue breaks into a chant:
Brahma Murari surachita lingam
nirmala bhasita shobhita lingam
janmaja dukkha vinashaka lingam
tat-pranamami Sadashiva lingam...

It's the Lingashtakam—an eight-stanza paean to Shiva's lingam, or phallus. I happen to know these opening lines by heart. They roughly translate to: 'I bow to the eternal Shiva lingam, which is adored by Brahma and Vishnu, which is pure, shining and bedecked, which destroys the sorrows that afflict us right from our birth.'

Like most prominent Hindu deities, Shiva too has been given a physical form: muscular; matted locks from which springs forth the Ganga; a cobra coiled around the neck; a crescent moon resting against the head; large, introspective eyes, a half-closed third eye. But he is almost always worshipped in the form of the lingam that is mounted on a base representing the yoni, or vulva.

The placing of the lingam on the yoni symbolises generative power—but isn't Shiva the god of destruction? It doesn't matter. For his devotees Shiva is capable of both: generating hope as well as destroying sorrow.

Then there are people like me, almost atheists, who are more groupies than devotees of this rock star of a god who makes vices look like virtues and who is as comfortable dwelling atop a pristine mountain as in an ash-laden cremation ground.

More than Shiva, it is the idea of Shiva in which I believe. Shiva's is an attitude you can aspire to. The day you walk around a cremation ground with the same sense of belonging that a young couple experiences on a tour of a house they expect to own soon, you've become Shiva.

At 2.45 the queue begins to inch forward. By the time I am inside the temple, after being frisked multiple times, it is well past three and the ritual has begun. The earliest to arrive are already seated right outside the sanctum sanctorum, in an area marked by steel benches. They are watching the proceedings without blinking, for a blink would cost them a fraction of a second of the holiest of sights. I join the crowd surrounding the steel benches and, standing on my toes, catch a glimpse of the lingam being decorated with flowers amidst chanting.

A portly, ponytailed Tamil in priest's robes, seated in the enclosed area, is so overcome by the spectacle that he decides to stand up and watch, blocking the view of a Bengali woman behind him. She instantly protests, '*Ei, kya karta hai?* Sit down! Sit down!' The man ignores her at first, but his flabby back is unable to withstand the fusillade of her angry words and he caves in.

Monkeys, meanwhile, go about their business, unimpressed by the ceremony. It is difficult to say whether their day is coming to an end or has just begun, but it is clear that the top half of all structures that constitute the temple belong to these simians. Some are walking on the ledges, with their little ones on their backs; some are half-asleep in the niches of the spires; some others are intently surveying the scene below, looking for goodies to grab.

The scene must not have been very different a hundred or even two hundred years ago. Way back in 1885, the *London Daily Telegraph* reported that a railway company had turned down a plea from the Brahmins of Banaras to transport 10,000 'superfluous' monkeys to faraway Saharanpur. The plea was made after two failed attempts by the king of Banaras to relocate the monkeys to the other side of the river, where his fort stood.

At present the lingam disappears under a mountain of marigold. The aarti, obeisance by oil lamps, begins. Those attending this pre-dawn ritual are entitled to a privilege extended to devotees only twice a day: touching of the lingam. So, while the aarti is still on, we are asked to queue up again. I think of the favours I need to ask of Shiva.

Standing in line, I hear a familiar voice behind me. I look back to find it belongs to the elderly Bengali woman who had quelled the Tamil priest. She is still querulous, complaining loudly to a female companion about the queue not moving. She is also calling out new arrivals attempting to sneak into the line ahead of us.

The lady has a fresh grouse: the wastage of milk. She had been at the temple the night before as well, to watch the closing ritual, and was appalled by the sight of milk—'pots of them'—being poured on the lingam. 'Imagine the number of children that could have been fed,' she complains.

Bells suddenly clang, drowning her whines. M.S. Subbulakshmi's *Suprabhatam* begins to play on the temple speakers. The time is 3.45. A new day has begun in Banaras. The queue begins finally to move. I wait for my turn to touch Shiva.

The mountain of marigold has been removed and the lingam is now bare and brown and glistening. Many devotees are so overwhelmed by the sight that they throw themselves over it and refuse to let go. They have to be forcibly lifted by the temple staff and shoved out of the door. To a monkey perched at a height, the scene would resemble a stampede.

I've barely felt the wet lingam when a strong arm grabs my shoulder: 'That's it, just one touch. Now move on!' My list of favours is not very long, but the time allotted to me turns out to be even shorter. Never mind. Shiva should know what's on my mind.

I walk in the direction of my lodge, barely a few hundred metres away, hidden in a riverside gali. Gali means an alley. Banaras, that is Kashi, is essentially a network of galis set against the ghats. I seem to be its sole inhabitant as I find my way back: hardly a soul around.

Soon, this timeless city will be up and about, the first light of the day unveiling the familiar silhouettes of parasols by the river and the boats on it. But for the moment, I feel Banaras belongs to me—and I belong to Banaras.

2.

THERE ARE TWO Banarases.

One is a geographical entity, India's holiest town, located in the state of Uttar Pradesh, peopled by pilgrims and tourists, pictures of its ghats instantly recognisable to anyone with the faintest knowledge of India. The other is a culture, a way of life, inhabited by citizens whose betel-stuffed mouths will tell you how foolish it is to chase material success at the cost of everlasting happiness.

In the first Banaras, if Shiva were to make a public appearance, people would instantly fall at his feet and beg for miracles. In the second, they would invite him to the nearest tea stall and ask him to share some of his wisdom.

After breakfast at the lodge I set out again, with no particular destination in mind. In Banaras, when you don't have a particular destination in mind, your feet invariably drag you towards the ghats. But first I need to fix my fountain pen—a Mont Blanc presented to me many years ago, my lucky charm—which, of late, has not been writing as smoothly as I would like it to. I step into Pen and Co., a shop I have been recommended, located on the road leading to the Dashashwamedha Ghat, and show it to Nishant, the young proprietor. The shop was started by his grandfather, in 1946.

Considering that many of the country's rich once maintained an additional home in Banaras, I am not surprised by the framed promotional posters of Mont Blanc and Sheaffer hanging on the walls. They were put up when fountain pens were commonly used and have remained there since. Nishant ruthlessly pulls out the nib and the feed from mine, drops them in a cup of water, scrubs them clean with a piece of cloth and puts them back in place. My Mont Blanc is writing like a gel pen.

'Good to see someone using a fountain pen in this day and age.' The remark comes from an old man dressed in a white shirt and dhoti, which match his venerable beard. He has come to the shop to make a pending payment.

'Where do you live?' I ask him.

'Very near here, in Vishwanath Gali.'

'You must be visiting the temple often.'

'Temple? What for! I last went there—wait, let me think—twenty-two years ago.'

'What prevents you?'

'Why should I go to the temple to see God? What's the point of praying to a stone? Do you actually get to see the Divine? For me, everybody is God. He (pointing to Nishant) is God, you are God, I am also God. Cleanse this first'—he taps his heart—'cleanse your thoughts, cleanse your actions and you won't need to go to a temple.'

Then he adds, with a mischievous smile: 'All these rich people, they come to the temple like beggars—they beg before Shiva. They are actually begging for destruction, because Shiva is the destroyer.'

'Nice meeting you, sir,' I say, when I sense our conversation is drawing to a close, 'but what is your name?'

The man laughs: '*Naam to sirf ek sanket hai, kya batana?*'—A name is merely for identification, how does it matter what it is?

'I would like to know.'

He thinks for a moment and says: 'Bholenath.'

Bholenath—lord of simplicity—is another name for Shiva.

3.

'FAKE SADHUS!' EXCLAIMS Dasu, the boatman. 'All fake sadhus, out to extort money from foreigners!'

Dasu and I, our acquaintance barely five minutes old, are surveying the Dashashwamedha Ghat. He had offered me a ride on the river, I had found the price too high, but we got talking. We are now looking at an ash-covered man, wearing saffron robes and a flowing white beard, posing against the river with his right palm held up in blessing while a Japanese tourist clicks away with her expensive camera.

Dasu says: 'Why would real sadhus loiter around here? They would be in caves and jungles. How can you be a sadhu when you are attracted to money? Money is the enemy of spirituality. You need just about enough money to eat three meals a day, and to educate your children. Hoarding money is not good for society. Money must keep circulating.'

'Will you take me to Assi Ghat?' I ask him.

He guides me down the steps to his rickety boat, but not before he has informed a well-fed man lounging on a cot: 'Going to Assi. 500 rupees.' Dasu tells me the man is his employer—the owner of the boat—who will keep 300 rupees and give him the rest.

Once we are on the river, the city of Banaras goes into mute mode. All I hear is the creaking of the oars and the slap of water against the sides of our boat—and the occasional shouted conversation of tourists on other boats.

I am not sure if my maternal grandfather, when he came here shortly before my birth, had taken a boat ride, but if he had, riverfront Banaras—a jumble of former palaces and temples—must have appeared to him just how it does to me now. Changes induced by time and technology are impossible to gauge midstream.

Halfway into the journey, Dasu takes off his shirt, carefully folds it and puts it aside. He has begun to sweat. Watching his wiry arms work the oars, I can't help think about the strangeness of the world we share: one in which the wealthy exercise so that they can burn what they've eaten, while the poor exercise so that they get to eat.

Against the green sunlit backdrop of the river, Dasu's features become clearer. I can now see the wrinkles and the strain. I feel like a heavy burden on his boat. On the brighter side, I am a source of his income. I try looking away, but my eyes keep returning to his sun-baked face—that's also because he is nearly always uttering something profound. Even now he is telling me something; I am not really listening to him, but I do register the words: 'Whoever is born has to die.'

'How old are you, Dasu?'

'I don't know, babu. All I know is that I was born a couple of years before the 1948 floods. My father died soon after I was born and I grew up at the home of my maternal uncle. Life was tough—you have no idea how tough it was. When I was old enough to work, I began working in a sari factory, weaving saris. Then I fell ill and my eyesight became weak and I could no longer weave saris. To weave saris you need sharp eyes. So I became a boatman. My wife is tenth-pass, but I am *angootha chhaap*, illiterate. I wasn't fit for any other job.'

'Do you have children?'

'I have three sons and two daughters. Except the youngest son, all are married.'

'Are your sons also boatmen?'

'No, I didn't want them to be. They work in shops. My job is fraught with uncertainties, you see. I hardly get any business during the monsoon and during peak summer months. But still, by the grace of Mother Ganga, I have been able to buy a small piece of land near Kashi station and have built a house there. I didn't have the money to instal windows, but I made sure the house had a door. Please come home sometime and take a meal with us.'

'I would love to, but tell me, don't you contemplate retirement?'

'My children ask me not to work. They say they will take care of me, but I don't like the idea of living off them. I need money for my daily expenses, and I cannot keep asking them for it. They will give me money for one day, for two days, maybe three days. On the fourth day, they will say to themselves, "He is asking for money every day!" I don't want that to happen. You want to get dropped off at Assi Ghat or do you want me to take you back to Dashashwamedha?'

'I want to get off at Assi.'

4.

VARANASI IS THE fusion of Varuna and Asi, the two rivers that meet the Ganga here, their confluences barely seven kilometres apart.

This seven-kilometre curve—its extremities marked by Rajghat (near the Varuna confluence) and Assi Ghat (near the Asi confluence)—forms the spinal cord of the city that has been in continuous existence for at least 3,000 years.

Present-day Banaras, however, is barely 300 years old, much of it built by the Marathas, even though Mark Twain was struck by its oldness during his visit in 1897, when the city had been younger by over a century: 'Banaras is older than history, older than tradition, older even than legend, and looks twice as old as all of them put together.'

In Banaras, how old is old depends on whether you are looking at its vintage in terms of the physical or metaphysical.

Assi Ghat, even though one of the oldest, looks the newest of the ghats, refurbished only recently by Prime Minister Narendra Modi, who represents Varanasi in Parliament. It's also one of the cleanest and most spacious, complete with a toilet complex and an open-air stage. Pilgrims rarely ever venture to this ghat, which serves more as a hangout for locals and also students of the nearby Banaras Hindu University, or BHU.

Sitting on a bench at Assi, I gaze at the river for a while. Then I have lunch in an open-air eatery called Pizzeria, though instead of pizza I have basmati rice along with arhar ki daal that is served in a miniature steel bucket. Adjacent to the eatery is Kashi Annapurna Book House where, to my utter delight, I find two copies of my first book, *Chai, Chai*. My mother had not lived to see the book: an advance copy had reached me eight days after I cremated her at Manikarnika.

I also find a number of books on Banaras; only one, the young man who runs the shop tells me, sells like hot cakes: Diana L. Eck's *Banaras—City of Light*. How should I make my Banaras book different so that it doesn't gather dust on his shelves? The thought weighs on my mind as I step out of the shop.

Not sure what to do next, I call up Amit Kumar, a local artist I've known only on Facebook and who had recommended the riverside lodge to me. He arrives on his motorcycle about thirty minutes later and together we stroll over to a nearby art gallery. Amit happens to know its owner, a garrulous man who tells me, over tea, that to find Banaras I must lose myself in the galis of Banaras. He also tells me that Banaras is the city of Shiva and here no one else—no matter how mighty—matters.

Soon we are joined by two men. More tea is ordered. One of the men is also an artist: a couple of his works hang in the gallery. The other man has just built a river ambulance which still doesn't have emergency-care equipment because of lack of funds. He suggests a ride in his ambulance. 'Some other day,' I tell him.

After spending close to two hours at the gallery—my pen has been used only once, to write the words, 'To find Banaras, lose yourself in the galis of Banaras'—I gesture to Amit that we should leave. The river-ambulance man follows us out of the door. He is begging me to take a ride. He wants me to write about his novel project in the newspaper so that it catches the attention of potential sponsors.

I ask Amit if he would like to come along, and since he is fine with the idea, I agree, reluctantly. The ambulance, it turns out, is moored at faraway Manikarnika. We set out on two motorcycles: the ambulance man insists I sit behind him, while the other artist rides pillion with Amit.

We manoeuvre through the heavy evening traffic, and by the time we enter the alley leading to Manikarnika, the sun has set. The familiar smell of burning hits my nostrils. We stand close to the pyres and watch a young, well-built boatman clad in jeans ready the river ambulance—basically a speedboat—for the ride. He is going to be our skipper.

Around seven o'clock, the four of us step onto the boat and for about thirty minutes go up and down the Ganga, as if we owned the river. I am glad I came—and I tell them so. The ambulance man suggests we have drinks. We pool in money and hand it to the skipper, who parks the boat at Harishchandra Ghat and jumps off. Making his way through two burning pyres, he disappears into an alley and emerges with a bottle of whisky and plastic glasses.

The ambulance man now directs the skipper to take the boat to the middle of the river and turn off the engine. 'Let it just float,' he declares, 'and let us enjoy.'

The artist opens the bottle, fills the cap with whisky and respectfully empties it over the river. 'The first drink must be offered to the Ganga,' he explains, 'that is the custom.' The plastic glasses are handed around and filled. 'Cheers!' we cry in delight.

Kashi means the City of Light. At this moment, it indeed is. There is light in the form of riverside halogen lamps, there is light in the form of pyres. These lights, the artificial as well as the natural, reflect on the river as wobbling, dazzling lines. And then there is the moon, large and red, rising from the white sands of the opposite bank.

As the alcohol enters our bloodstream, secrets begin to pour out—secrets about Banaras that, I am told, I wouldn't find on the internet or in any book. Almost every sentence spilling out of the mouths of the ambulance man and the artist is prefaced with: 'No one knows about this yet.' One secret is foreign women wanting to make babies with the men of Banaras, who have superior genes.

The skipper, who has not been offered a drink, says he has slept with two Israeli and two Japanese women. I ask him if he has ever encountered aghoris, the reclusive sadhus who, in their pursuit of conquering fear and disgust, spend time in cremation grounds and are known even to consume the flesh of the dead.

'I haven't seen them in a long time. One night, some years ago, I did see a few aghoris—I think they were from Tamil Nadu—camped right across Manikarnika. They were chanting some strange mantra that attracted the dead bodies floating in the river. They dragged the bodies ashore. I did not have the courage to watch after that.'

'Is it common to find bodies floating in the river?' I ask him.

'Not common,' he replies, 'but not uncommon either. Hindus don't cremate five kinds of dead: those who die of snakebite; those who die of burns; those who die of small pox; pregnant women; and sadhus. Their bodies are consigned whole to the river.'

I wonder what if, in a setting so perfect—on one side of the river the moonlit sands and on the other the ancient city, and we on a river that is no ordinary river—a body happens to brush against the boat? As I picture the macabre sight, I am interrupted by the artist: 'We are giving you such a good time. What do we get in return?'

An awkward silence grips the boat. What irritates me more is his cocky expression. I want to tell him the ride wasn't my idea, but I realise that I am their prisoner, and mumble something about giving publicity to their noble project.

The ambulance man, sensing my discomfort, changes the subject. He points to the moonlit bank and says, 'The sand has been freshly deposited by the river. It is so fine that your feet will sink as soon as you step onto it.' He directs the skipper to turn on the engine and soon we hit the bank and hop off the boat, one at a time.

This side of the river, an integral part of the Banaras landscape, is technically Ramnagar. Once upon a time, the ambulance man tells me, the well-to-do people of Banaras used this vast stretch of sand as an open-air toilet. Every morning they would take the boat across the river to take a leisurely dump and return to the city purified and happy after a dose of bhang.

We pee on the sands, after which I break away from the rest to gaze at the red moon and take pictures. My phone, to my disappointment, is unable to capture what my eyes see. I feel a hand on my shoulder. It is the river-ambulance man. 'Spectacular, isn't it? I am so glad you came.' And then, clearing his throat: 'Dada, I spent 2,800 rupees on diesel for this trip. Would you mind paying that amount—and maybe a small tip for the boatman so that he can buy himself a bottle of liquor?'

I have sensed this coming. I tell him I don't have the cash, and that I will have to visit the ATM. He protests politely, 'When did I say you have to pay me right away?'

All the pleasurable moments I've earned go down the Ganga. With money weighing on my mind, I miss a step while climbing onto the boat and land on the wet soil of the river.

It is almost eleven in the night when we get back on the motorcycles at Manikarnika, my left foot now mud-caked. The ambulance man again insists I sit behind him—we have to go to the ATM. Amit and the artist will follow us.

In one of the alleys leading out of Manikarnika, he stops the vehicle and tilts it—we tilt our torsos as well—to give an incoming funeral procession right of way: '*Ram naam satya hai*!' Once the procession has gone past, the ambulance man tries to kick-start the engine but the machine is now as lifeless as the man on the bier that has just gone past. The ambulance man is distraught. Amit and the artist catch up with us. They all examine the dead motorbike.

The ambulance man and the artist decide to spend the night at Manikarnika. They will sleep in the river ambulance. I can see resignation in the eyes of the ambulance man as he drags his vehicle in the reverse direction. I climb onto Amit's motorcycle and we drive out to the main road where we have dinner in a restaurant that is still open. He feels sorry for me, I feel sorry for him.

After dinner, since there is not even a cycle-rickshaw in sight, he decides to drop me to the lodge. The lodge is still about a kilometre away when he has a flat tire. 'I am sorry, you will have to find your way back.' Amit is apologetic, as if the fault is his. 'Don't worry about me,' he adds, 'I will find a safe place to leave the bike and then go home.'

It feels heartless to leave him like that, but there is very little I can do, other than giving him the option of spending the night with me, but he says he must get back home.

I walk back to the lodge and find the gate latched. I knock and knock until, about twenty minutes later, the cook peers down from the terrace. Another ten minutes before he climbs down to noisily open the latch. I go to the bathroom to wash the mud off my foot, but the tap is dry. I go to bed complete with the mud-caked foot, comforting myself with the thought that this is no ordinary mud but a blessing from the Ganga.

5.

BANARAS, IT IS said, rests on the trident of Shiva. It surely rests on a trident whose three prongs are fact, fiction and faith.

My personal theory is that Banaras is Banaras because of its location. Here, the east-bound Ganga snakes northward, as a result of which the city wakes up to an orange ball rising right across the river and thus gets to watch—and worship—the two most powerful elements of nature in a single frame, one brilliantly illuminating the other. This spectacle probably attracted the first settlers and that's how Banaras came into being—as simple as that.

But perhaps it isn't as simple as that. The devout will insist that the Ganga chooses to take a northward curve at Banaras only because it is Banaras. God created man or man created God—the jury will be out until the end of time. At the moment, though, day is breaking and I am walking along the river. I can hear the call of the muezzin. I can also hear a boatman sing to the two Westerners on his boat. I have no knowledge of ragas but his rendition—raw and uninhibited—tears through the morning air, giving me goosebumps. My eyes now meet those of a priest who is setting up shop under a giant parasol. I stop to ask him how he believes Banaras came into being.

'Shiva and Parvati,' he tells me, 'needed a place to spend their leisure time, so Shiva created Kashi and placed it on his trident. In fact, the entire universe rests on his trident, and it is Kashi that is in direct contact with it.'

Just when I wonder whether Shiva created Kashi out of thin air, the priest adds, 'He chose this spot to spend his leisure time because back then this was a beautiful, fragrant forest called Anand Kaanan, full of sandalwood trees, close to which was a maha shamshaan (major cremation ground), called the Manikarnika. As you know, Shiva likes to live close to cremation grounds, so he made himself comfortable in Kashi.'

'So Manikarnika predates Shiva's Kashi?'

'Not just Manikarnika. There is a pond called Pishach Mochan, where people have been performing rituals for the dead since time immemorial—that too was in existence before Shiva created Kashi.'

So, going by his story, humans inhabited Banaras—people were being born and were living and dying—even before Shiva decided to set up home here. Who created those humans? Did they ever bump into Shiva? Did Shiva announce to them that he was going to create a new city in their settlement? I am sure the answers exist, though the stories may vary.

I am now at Darbhanga Ghat, having tea out of a paper cup and watching the sun rise. The sunrise in Banaras is a picture-postcard one: that's an unquestionable fact, not a story.

6.

SEATED ON A barber's chair at the Dashashwamedha Ghat is a bearded white man having his head shaved, surrounded by a semi-circle of Indians watching him with their mouths open.

The barber finally holds a smaller mirror behind the shining pate so that the white man can see, in the larger mirror, what a neat job he has done. The client gives his reflection the thumbs-up, pays and walks away.

The barber runs behind him, holding up two torn twenty-rupee notes: 'Sir! Sir! Very mistake! *Very* mistake!' Relieved when the foreigner promptly replaces the torn notes, he says: 'Next time, beard shave! I give you good service.'

The semi-circle, which has followed the barber, disperses now.

India is a country of bystanders. What's going on?—nowhere else does this question arouse so much curiosity as in this part of the world. And in Banaras, something is always going on. Only that here, because of the halo that hangs over its ghats, even the mundane can be a spectacle: such as the sight of a white man getting his head tonsured. Replace him with an Indian and you still have the ingredients for a jaw-dropping picture worth sharing on Instagram. Banaras may not be beautiful, but it is photogenic.

My days quickly acquire a pattern. I begin to wake up before daybreak to watch sunrise from either Dashashwamedha Ghat or the nearby Darbhanga Ghat and return to the lodge for breakfast on its terrace, where tourists are nearly always to be seen rolling their weed or heard planning trips to—invariably—Jaipur.

After breakfast I walk, ghat to ghat, from Dashashwamedha right up to Assi, where I kill time mostly doing nothing. Sometimes I climb up the steps to the Kashi Annapurna Book House to look at the books on Banaras, only to be intimidated by their contents: the threads connecting the existence of the city to the ancient texts are woven far more complexly than its galis. Still, I like to linger in the shop because its glass panels offer a magnificent view of Assi and the river.

Around lunchtime, I take a cycle-rickshaw back to Godowlia, the bustling intersection near Dashashwamedha, where I eat in one of the restaurants only if I am very hungry. Then I laze in the lodge, and re-emerge around 4.30 to spend some time at Dashashwamedha before settling myself down at Darbhanga Ghat.

I have become very fond of Darbhanga Ghat. Set against a sandstone palace more than a hundred years old, it has neither the crowds of Dashashwamedha nor the calm of Assi, but is a lively place that gives you a grandstand view of riverside Banaras without your having to be a part of the bustle.

One evening, on the marhi at Darbhanga Ghat—marhis are octagonal platforms, of varying height and girth, dotting the ghats of Banaras—I find an unusual mix of people seated in a circle. There is a white sadhu, there are two Indian sadhus, there is a boy ascetic (an apprentice of one of the Indian sadhus), and there is a young Japanese couple with their child, a boy of about seven or eight. A chillum is being passed around. Everyone, except the two boys, take drags in turns.

With some hesitation, I climb up the steps of the marhi and join the circle. I am offered a drag but I decline. The Japanese couple appears to be in a trance: they assume a devotee-like expression each time they put the chillum to the lips. I ask them what brings them to Banaras. It is the woman who replies, almost choking with emotion, 'In Japan, life is full of stress. Here'—she taps the floor of the marhi—'I feel the stress leaving my body.' The child watches his mother with a blank expression. This is their second visit to Banaras and certainly not the last, considering that the city has turned out to be a spa for their minds.

I turn to the Indian sadhus. We make small talk. I am served some food for thought:

'Everything is for the time being, isn't it?'

'*Dimag, dil aur ling*—head, heart and dick—when they synchronise, you become Shiva.'

'*Yaar bichhad jaaye toh sanam kya kare, maut aa jaye to bhagwan kya kare?*'—What can you do if your beloved is gone; likewise, what can God do if death comes knocking?

I tell the sadhus that I have never seen a white sadhu before and ask them if I can have a chat with him. The white sadhu looks at me and says that he isn't white but very much Indian. His grandfather was a Marwari who had married a French woman in Pondicherry and their son—the sadhu's father—married a Punjabi.

'My name is Amrit Das Phawrawala,' he tells me. 'Phawrawala means the one who wields the phawra, or hoe. This is not the name my parents gave me—that name doesn't matter anymore.

'I was born in Pondicherry in 1943, when it was still ruled by the French. I studied in Lawrence School in Sanawar, and then studied medicine for two years in Ajmer.

'I dropped out of medical school because I wanted to be a designer. I had inherited my grandmother's taste in stylish clothes. I settled in Pushkar as a successful designer; the later group of hippies—the ones who came to India in the 1970s—wore clothes I designed.

'Then one day I went to the Ujjain kumbh with my family. There I met a guru and was so influenced by him that I decided to give it all up and become a sadhu. Eventually, I moved to Nepal and lived there for close to twenty years, spending about ten years in Mustang and three in Waling.

'You know why the place is called Waling? That's because, about 150 years ago, a one-armed sadhu from Andhra Pradesh arrived there. He had a huge penis and when the local people saw him they exclaimed, "*Wah ling!*" I was in Waling when, in 2013, I set out for India to attend the maha kumbh at Allahabad, but my bike rolled off the mountain and I was badly hurt, so I had to stay on. It's only three months since I have been in India. Let's see how long I stay on.'

'How has India changed from the time you left?'

'It has changed a lot! Back then it was a nation of beggars, now it isn't.'

Aimless in Banaras

The sun has set. The river is teeming with boats, the ghats with people. One of the Indian sadhus sitting with me suddenly decides to add colour to the twilight. He stands up, drops the cloth around his waist and lifts his hands high up in prayer. Chanting a salutation, he rotates 360 degrees with his hands held up, giving Banaras a glimpse of his penis and ash-coated butt.

Once he is seated, the other Indian sadhu stands up. He picks up a stick, wraps his penis around it and makes a knot. He then signals the boy sadhu to climb over his back and stand on the stick. The boy obeys him, and for a few moments, his entire weight is borne by his senior's penis.

The Japanese couple watches the demonstration in a daze. They've just witnessed the load-carrying capacity of the lingam. Will the man seek to replicate the trick once back home in Japan?

Climbing down the marhi, I am accosted by a young boatman. He is actually a boy of fourteen. His name is Rahul. I turn down his offer for a ride but he appears keen on having a conversation. He asks me the kind of questions grownups usually come up with: whether I was married, whether I had kids, the purpose of my visit to Banaras.

'Oh, you are doing a book on Banaras!' the boy exclaims. 'Then you must speak to that man.'

'Which man?'

'That man standing over there with a foreigner. He is from Banaras, and the foreigner is his wife, from Canada.'

'What does he do?'

'As far as I know, nothing. She came to study in Banaras and fell in love with him.'

'Will they talk to me?'

'Why don't you find out?'

I walk over to the couple and find myself stunned for a moment: she is the most beautiful white woman I've *ever* seen. Hoping for a lengthy interview, I introduce myself to—of course—the man.

'Let's meet another day so that we can have a long chat,' the man dismisses me. 'Banaras is a complex subject which can take many lifetimes to understand.'

The woman does not even look at me. A faint smile adorns her perfect lips and her gaze is fixed on the river.

7.

BANARAS IS AN open book. You can turn its pages, go through the sentences and paragraphs over and over again, read between the lines if you like, and yet it is unlikely that you will fully grasp the city.

If you lay any claim to understanding it, there will always be a Banarasi lying in wait to counter your every assumption: 'No, you don't understand it well enough, yet. Let *me* tell you what Banaras is all about.' And then he will offer you a seat, order tea and hold you prisoner to a long-drawn conversation.

That's at least one thing I've understood about Banaras: its people are generally averse to being subjected to a quick question-and-answer session; they would rather have a conversation that allows them to share, at a leisurely pace, the wisdom they've acquired over the years from various sources. I have even met Banarasis who've asked me to stop taking notes and instead 'lose myself' in the conversation, but right now I am with a Banarasi who is insisting that I write down what he tells me.

I bumped into this stranger outside a timber mart, not very far from Assi Chauraha, and when he learned that I had come to write about the city, he congratulated me profusely. Just to let him know that I was not entirely new to Banaras, I told him that I had cremated my mother at Manikarnika as recently as 2009.

'Oh really? Kala Bhairava would have sent her straight to heaven,' he remarked.

'Who's Kala Bhairava?'

'The angry version of Shiva, didn't you know?'

He then half-dragged me to a hardware shop next door and, without the shopkeeper's permission, installed me on a plastic chair there. 'Write down the 108 names of Kala Bhairava,' he is ordering me now.

After jotting down about twenty names, I put my foot down. 'Sir, these names are not relevant to my work on Banaras.'

'But do you even know who allowed you to come to Banaras?'

'Who?'

'Lord Ganesha, who else! There are fifty-six Ganeshas in Banaras, each with a different name. Now write down those names.'

I have no choice but to once again put my fountain pen to paper. He means well and I don't wish to offend him. But he himself doesn't remember all the names: he recites them by rote and, from time to time, shuts his eyes and chants the same mantra over and again until he has produced around fifty.

'I may have missed a few names,' he confesses. 'If they don't add up to fifty-six, do not worry, call me any time and I shall supply you with the missing names. Note down my phone number.'

I do as asked.

'Other than madam, no one else has this number. I have another number as well, note that down too.'

'Which madam, sir?'

'Sonia Gandhi, who else! She is soon going to induct me into the All-India Congress Committee. You are the first person in the whole of Banaras to know this.'

That I am the only person to be privy to a secret about Banaras—I have been accorded this privilege more times than I can count.

8.

AT 9 O'CLOCK in the evening, Dashashwamedha Ghat is bathed in light and throbbing with life. The boats have been moored for the night. Temple bells are tinkling. Pilgrims are playing tourists. Boys are playing cricket in various corners, their bats crude and stumps made up of bricks. There are sadhus all around, smeared with ash, going about their business—such as it is. The wooden cots used by priests during the day are now occupied by locals. Some locals are walking their dogs. One of the books I had leafed through at the Assi Ghat bookshop had called Dashashwamedha the Piccadilly of Banaras: the comparison seems apt at this hour.

I find myself space on one of the cots, to give my back a rest, little knowing that I am actually joining a group of friends who meet at the ghat every evening. The group includes a rice merchant, a vegetable vendor, a furniture-seller, a hosiery retailer, and a priest.

The vegetable vendor says, 'We meet here every evening, come what may. This is how we relax our minds. If we didn't come here, we'd fall ill.'

The rice merchant adds dolefully, 'Banaras isn't what it used to be. The culture is changing. These days, boys don't even shave their heads when the occasion demands. They are too much into fashion.'

The furniture-seller embarks on an opposite tack: 'Kids are different nowadays. They don't even let us use cusswords. Even if I say something as simple as *bhosrikay*, they say, "Papa, don't use bad words." Come on, this is Banaras! Cusswords are a way of life for us.'

The hosiery retailer says, 'The kids stay glued to their phones. When we were that young, we would save money all year round so that we could spend it at the Ram Lila. Have you been to the Ram Lila yet? Oh, you must go there one of these evenings—the performances have already begun for this year. They are staged on the other side of the river, at different venues around the Ramnagar Fort.'

The priest says, 'Yes, the children must know their culture. They should know they live in a great country that is blessed by gods. Tell me one thing: we have crores of gods and goddesses, why did all of them make India their home? Why did they not choose to live in America or Japan or Australia? Do you have an answer?'

The next afternoon, eager to watch the Ram Lila, I take a boat from Assi Ghat to the fort situated diagonally across the river.

Ram Lila, the enactment of Lord Rama's life as described in Tulsidas's *Ramcharitmanas*, typically takes place over the nine nights preceding Dussehra. But in Banaras—where the Ram Lila is said to have originated, during Tulsidas's lifetime—performances are spread over a month, without the aid of electric lights or loudspeakers.

In most other towns though, loudspeakers are liberally used. I've never watched the Ram Lila before even though

I've grown up in north India, but my ears have often caught snatches of the *Ramcharitmanas* wafting through autumn nights from a makeshift stage in some remote corner of the neighbourhood we lived in. I even knew a man who played Hanuman every year but I never got around to watching him perform.

The boatman taking me to the fort turns out, once again, to be elderly. Even though the fare he had quoted seemed steep for a ride just across the river, I had agreed without a murmur because I've resolved not to haggle with elderly boatmen.

'I will show you something,' he says as he rows upstream, keeping the boat close to the riverbank. Cutting diagonally across the river can be strenuous if the destination is upstream, so boatmen, as a practice, skirt the bank until the destination is downstream and then cross over with ease.

Upstream of Assi is something that appears to be a ghost ghat—there's not a human in sight. The boatman identifies it for me: 'This is Ravidas Ghat, built by Mayawati when she was the chief minister (of Uttar Pradesh).' Banaras, quite clearly, is not receptive to anything that doesn't go back to the time of the gods.

Beyond Mayawati's ghat is wild, uncultivated ground. I spot a kingfisher perched on a mound. 'Now you will see what I wanted to show you,' the boatman says. A moment ago I was taking pictures of the kingfisher, and now I am staring at the mouth of a drain.

'The filth produced by the whole of Banaras gushes out of this every morning, at around 5.30 or six,' he says. 'That is why you should never bathe in the river in the mornings. We are poor and illiterate, but we never throw even a piece of paper or a banana peel into the river, because the river is our source of income. But look at how the people of Banaras treat their river—and they worship the same river.'

We have been on the boat for nearly thirty minutes now, but the fort looks just as distant as it had from Assi Ghat. Looks can indeed be deceptive. I feel glad I hadn't bargained with the boatman.

Once we have left the drain way behind and are almost in the middle of the river, he says, 'Now you can dip your hand in the water and sprinkle a few drops on your head. You will earn the blessings of Mother Ganga.'

On the opposite bank, which is growing closer now, a man in his underwear is vigorously scrubbing down one of his many buffaloes. Dirty river, squeaky-clean buffaloes—welcome to India.

Finally, the sandstone fort, which has been a hazy image for me all these days, stands etched before me as if close enough to touch. The boatman advises me how to get back in the night, when I am unlikely to find a boat—he is shouting out various options to me even after I have paid him and started walking away in the direction of the fort.

At the museum in the fort, I find myself admiring vintage cars, palanquins, elephant howdahs, and antique weapons. Then, standing on a balcony overlooking the river, I watch the sun—a large, luminescent orange plate—lower itself behind the buildings of Banaras.

Wandering out of the fort I enter the bustle of Ramnagar town. A young pani-puri seller is busy squeezing a handful of tamarind in a jar filled with water. Once the water has acquired the flavour of the tamarind, he adds the condiments to it. The concoction that causes a tangy explosion in your mouth when you eat a pani-puri is ready—he has taken nearly thirty minutes to prepare it. I've had pani-puris all my life but have never watched the preparation of this all-important liquid. Vendors don't usually do it in public, and the unscrupulous ones, I am told, use acid instead of tamarind to lend the sour taste to the water. Needless to say, I become the young man's first customer of the evening.

I ask him for directions to the venue of the Ram Lila. He says the venue keeps changing—different venues for different episodes. This evening, the show is happening at—he names a ground. I hire an autorickshaw to get there and also make a deal with the driver for a drop back to Banaras once the show has ended.

The venue is the scene of a village fair. A few thousand people sit in an open ground facing a stage lit with gas lamps. Policemen are around, so are hawkers selling eatables. Seated on the stage, cross-legged and expressionless, are three children representing Ram, Laxman and Sita. There seems to be a break between scenes because villagers are climbing up onto the stage, three to four people at a time, to prostrate themselves before the children and to garland them. A garland-seller is seated by the steps leading to the dais: he will be richer by a few thousand rupees before the night comes to an end.

I buy two portions of warm, roasted groundnuts—one is for the driver—and try to imagine how electrifying the atmosphere must have been, say, forty autumns ago, when performances such as this were the sole source of relief from the annual grind. Television must have robbed the occasion of some of its magic, and now there is the smartphone—the biggest-ever distraction afflicting mankind—which would have surely diminished the appetite for such traditional forms of entertainment. Even a sunrise or sunset is no longer relished by the eyes; it is instead captured on the phone. Several attempts are made to get the perfect shot and by then the sun has either risen too high or disappeared behind the horizon.

Yet, such distractions have not been able to dilute the devotion, evident from the unending stream of people climbing onto the stage to seek the blessings of the children. They are no ordinary children. Since they are playing Ram, Sita and Laxman, they *are* real deities at this hour. The groundnut-seller, an old man, has probably read my thoughts. He observes: 'If people can pray to stone idols, why can't they pray to living beings playing gods and goddesses?'

I move closer to the stage to take pictures of the child-gods, but my view is invariably blocked by seekers of divine blessings. I have barely managed to take a couple of pictures when a police officer menacingly marches in my direction to tell me that photography is prohibited here. I am now surrounded by villagers who want a look at the pictures I've taken; they want me to forward the pictures to them so that they can store the images of the child-gods on their phones.

I extricate myself from the throng and return to the groundnut-seller to buy some more of his ware. I ask him if he has any idea when the next scene might start.

'My guess is as good as yours, but when a scene is about to begin, you will hear someone shout the warning, "*Chup raho! Saavdhaan!*"'

Time passes, but I hear no such warning. Who knows if what's going on now on the stage—the three children seated cross-legged and people seeking their blessings—is actually part of a longish episode? Soon I run out of groundnuts and also my patience. I tell the driver to take me back to Banaras. It's a beautiful October evening: I would rather sit on the ghat or have a drink in the lodge.

Ramnagar and Banaras, two towns on the opposite sides of the Ganga: one is a settlement, the other a civilisation.

9.

AIMLESS IN BANARAS—my heart says this should be the title of this book because it aptly describes my days in this eternal city, though it is likely that my head will think up something pretentious by the time the proofs are out.

There are books and there are books. One is an afterthought, when you look back at a segment of your life to realise you've accumulated sufficient material; the other is planned, when you already have a subject in mind and then set out to fill the pages with people and places.

But even planned books rarely go as per plan. I've so far written four books about places, and in each case the final manuscript has vastly differed from the initial synopsis submitted to the publisher—the difference reflecting the expanded horizons of the writer in the course of his research.

I have no idea if my wanderings around Banaras, a city still largely unknown to me, is broadening my horizons; all I can see on the horizon, no matter on which ghat I am, is the sands of Ramnagar. I have no list of people to meet, no particular places to visit, I am taking things as they come. To have a plan is to be distracted from Banaras, whose heart beats at a leisurely rhythm, best palpated with aimless walks along its ghats.

This afternoon, wandering into Darbhanga Ghat—I invariably find myself gravitating there—I spot the Pondicherry-born sadhu, whom I had mistaken for a white ascetic. He is dusting pigeon feed off a marhi—not the same marhi where I first met him—and when I walk up to him, he recognises me.

'How is Banaras treating you?' he asks me.

'So far, so good,' I tell him. 'How about you?'

'I have not been well for the past few days. I have been falling over. I am getting old, you see. I am going to sleep now. Sleep takes care of most illnesses.'

'Where are you going to sleep?'

'Right here. That's my bedding,' he points to a rolled up mat, which he is about to spread on the marhi.

'How long are you going to stay in Banaras?'

'I have no idea. But I would like to stay on in one place, preferably in a warm place, because I am getting old. The Himalayas are too cold for me now.'

'Have you any thoughts of God?'

'No, God doesn't matter much. No connections, no attachments, no duties except to look after yourself—those are all that matter.'

10.

ONE AFTERNOON, AFTER lunch at Assi Ghat, I decide to walk all the way to Rajghat, the opposite end of the chain of ghats.

As I walk, I still feel I am encountering the ghats for the first time. Each presents a different sight. Boys playing cricket. Boys flying kites. A lone boy seated on a ledge, his elbows resting on his knees, looking forlorn—Banarasis believe that sitting on the ghat can take away your worries. Washed clothes spread out to dry. Buffaloes being bathed. A man washing his bicycle in the river. Men soaping themselves standing in the water. Sadhus wandering in search of something that still eludes them. Tourists wandering in search of sadhus. One sadhu discreetly combing his hair. Two baby goats climbing up a marhi in clear defiance of their mother. A ram necking a dog. And then, as I get closer to Dashashwamedha, I become one of the many.

At Dashashwamedha, I pause for a paan. The delicious concoction has barely melted in my mouth when I order two more before continuing onward. I climb the steps leading to the Nepali Temple at Lalita Ghat. The temple, built some two centuries ago by the ruler of Nepal, offers a commanding view of the river. It is deserted at the moment, the perfect place to meditate.

Then the Manikarnika—ah, the all-too-familiar sights and smells! A part of me never wants to return here, but another part of me finds comfort in its surroundings.

Further on, very high on the wall of the large palace that marks the Bhonsale Ghat, I notice a crudely painted piece of information. The few words in Hindi demarcate a tragedy: 'In 1978, the water rose to this level'.

At Panchganga Ghat, I climb the steep incline of steps to the shrine of Trailanga Swami—described by the nineteenth-century mystic Ramakrishna Paramhansa as the Walking Shiva of Banaras—who, it is believed, lived for close to 300 years, spending the latter half of his life in Banaras, from 1737 to 1887. In the shrine is a large lingam which the swami is said to have extracted single-handedly from the bottom of the river and brought ashore, and a black life-size statue of the swami himself, depicted in the meditative pose.

I'd been to this temple before, the day after I had cremated my mother, and this time I see something new: there is an additional statue—of a Brahmin lost deep in meditation—facing that of the swami. Unlike the swami's statue, which has been chiselled out of black stone, this one looks strangely lifelike, straight out of Madame Tussauds.

Even as I am regarding the two statues, standing alone in the silence of the shrine, the eyes of the meditating Brahmin snap open. Startled, I step back.

'By any chance are you Mr Ghosh from Chennai?'

'I am.'

The man I mistook for a sculptor's creation now gets up to extend his hand: 'I am also from Chennai. I follow your column in the paper. We are also friends on Facebook.'

Mr Seshadri and I shake hands—we promise to meet again in Chennai—and I continue my walk in the direction of Rajghat. But I find my resolve to traverse the entire seven-kilometre stretch weakening. There is something depressing about the ghats that lie north of Dashashwamedha. They are poorly maintained—most of the time I am walking on mounds of silt—and deserted. This segment is also Banaras, but this is not where all the action takes place. I feel like a man who has an invitation to a garden party but, while finding his way to the garden, has strayed into wild vegetation.

Above all, the light is fading. The sky is already a pale shade of crimson, dotted with two flying kites. Finally, at Prahlad Ghat, I decide to call it a day. I approach a group of local men flocked by the river to ask them about the nearest exit to the main road, so that I can get a ride back to Dashashwamedha.

The oldest of them, raising his chin so that the juice of the paan in his mouth doesn't spill out, advises me: 'Why do you want to take the road? The jam will be terrible at this hour. We will get you a boat.'

Soon a motorised boat, large enough to seat fifty people, materialises. It is being steered by a boy who gives his age as thirteen but looks way younger.

'Do you go to school?' I ask him once we are on course.

He doesn't hear me. His mind—and eyes—are elsewhere. They are fixed on a kite whose string has just been snapped and which is now wafting down the sky in our direction. The boy is running around the boat to be in a position to grab it. The kite's descent is zigzag: one moment it appears within reach, the very next moment it drifts away, only to swing back in the direction of the boat.

The kite eventually lands on water, way beyond grabbing distance. 'Oh no,' the boy laughs.

'Do you go to school?' I ask again.

'Yes.'

'Which class are you in?'

'Third standard.'

In the fading light, the waters darkening, I spot something bobbing, not very far from the boat. It appears to me a genderless human face: features intact but skin peeled off. To be doubly sure it is a cadaver, I draw it to the attention of the boy. He reverently touches his right index finger to his forehead and chest and says, matter-of-factly: '*Laas hai, laas.*' He means laash: corpse.

Whose remains is the river carrying away? Did he or she drown, or was the body consigned to the river after death? If drowned—how? If consigned to the river—why? The answers will never be known. The corpse is just a drop in the ocean of mysteries the river holds in its bosom.

11.

'*MAADARCHOD!*'—MOTHER-FUCKER!

The voice belongs to the manager of the lodge. His outburst has woken me.

Curious to see who the recipient of his anger could be, I pull open the door slightly to find him yelling on the phone: '*Hum tumhari gaand mein namak mirch thhoos denge!*'—I will shove salt and chilli up your ass!

Noticing me, he breaks into a smile and asks, 'How do you find Banaras?'

'Just as I had expected,' I reply.

Like the juice of the paan, cusswords too are always brimming in the mouth of a Banarasi, waiting to be spat out. The recipient or the listener is rarely ever offended. I had thought my cussword-hardened ears had heard it all, but the other day, while travelling on a cycle-rickshaw from Assi to Dashashwamedha, they picked up an epithet new to me: *randiput*—son of a whore.

'We have idlis for breakfast today,' the manager tells me companionably.

'Really?'

'Yes. You must try the south Indian food of Banaras. Tastes any day better than the food you get in your south India.'

'Can I have breakfast in my room today?'

'By all means,' he replies jovially, and once the food arrives, invites himself into my room to have his tea while I eat.

The manager is an agreeable man, but I generally try to avoid him because eye contact invariably sparks off a prolonged conversation. Sometimes he barges into my room with the newspaper held open, exclaiming, '*Dekhiye aaj kya chhapa hai* (read this piece of news),' and we spend the next thirty to forty minutes discussing the state of the nation and, sometimes, the world.

This morning, though, he is holding forth on Banaras.

'What is Banaras? Banaras is *bana ras*, juice that is ready. Keep sipping on the juice, sir. Keep sipping!'

I put a piece of sambar-soaked idli in my mouth.

'We Banarasis believe in *khao, piyo, mast raho*'—eat, drink, be happy. 'Life is too short to be spent worrying.'

'You are right.'

'I am sure you would have heard this popular saying about Banaras: *Raand, saand, seerhi, sanyasi, inse bache to seve Kashi.*'

Raand stands for a widow who isn't old and is not averse to sexual liaisons, saand is a bull, seerhi is a flight of stairs, and sanyasi is an ascetic, a sadhu. Only if you guard yourself against these four—according to the saying—can you enjoy Kashi.

Saand, seerhi, sanyasi—these I come across on a daily basis and I am yet to fall victim to any of them. I haven't yet encountered a raand, though: for that, I guess, one needs to be living in Banaras and not merely losing oneself in its lanes.

12.

ONE AFTERNOON, SOON after my arrival in Banaras, I had met Rana P.B. Singh, who was kind enough to spare a couple of hours for me. Once the meeting ended, I realised the time could have been better invested reading him. This now-retired BHU professor's name is on the spine of nearly half the books about Banaras that sit on the shelves at the Kashi Annapurna Book House.

But one fact he had drawn my attention to remains in my head: that a large part of the Banaras seen today was built by two women—the Maratha queen Ahilyabai Holkar and a benevolent Bengali zamindar called Rani Bhabani. They were not only contemporaries but also happened to die in the same year, 1795, when Ahilyabai was seventy and Rani Bhabani seventy-nine.

It was Ahilyabai who reconstructed the Vishwanath Temple after it had been demolished by Mughal Emperor Aurangzeb—the gold for its spire and dome was later donated by Maharaja Ranjit Singh of Punjab. She built some of the other temples as well and also laid out some of the most prominent ghats, including the Dashashwamedha and Manikarnika.

Rani Bhabani, on her part, built water bodies, roads and temples—not just in Banaras but also across Bengal. She was so giving, it is said, that by the time she died she owned nothing except the sari she was wearing at the time.

The city also happens to be associated with another woman enshrined in Indian history, Rani Lakshmibai, who was born in the neighbourhood of Assi.

And yet Banaras remains a man's domain. It is men who mostly people its streets. It is men who exchange thoughts and cusswords over tea at the riverside or roadside stalls. It is men who can be seen seeking respite from daily life by lounging on the ghats in the evenings, having downed their daily quota of bhang. Where are the women? They are there, of course—in the kitchen, in the courtyard, on the terrace. You can't see them, but they can see you.

This evening, however, I run into a small gathering that consists of nearly as many women as men at the Prabhu Ghat, not very far from Assi. During my daily walks I always pause at this ghat because it is exceptionally clean and at the same time deserted: the perfect place to spend a few moments in reflection.

Some of the men are carrying guitars. Loudspeakers are being set up and standees erected. A musical programme is about to begin. It turns out that a radio channel is celebrating the first anniversary of a weekly show in which budding singers from the city are invited to perform, and many of the featured singers are now in attendance.

In the crowd, one woman stands out, not so much because of her appearance but because every now and then, someone or the other, mostly young men, is touching her feet.

'Who is she?' I ask a loitering boatman.

'She is from Nagaland. She is the one who cleaned up this ghat, all by herself.'

'Why, was this ghat dirty?'

'You can't even imagine how dirty. Go talk to her.'

Cleanliness has been a watchword in Banaras ever since its current representative in Parliament, Narendra Modi, shortly after he became the prime minister in May 2014, launched the countrywide Swachh Bharat—Clean India—campaign. In Banaras he chose Assi Ghat to set an example, and sanctioned close to 30 crore rupees for its cleaning and beautification. Men are still at work there, dislodging silt from the steps of the ghat with hosepipes. Initially, earthmovers were used for the purpose, but the machines—being machines—could not distinguish between silt and stone and ended up damaging some of the marhis.

The transformation of Prabhu Ghat shows that the bare hands of a determined citizen can be more capable than government machinery. The Naga lady is exchanging pleasantries with the other invitees when I introduce myself to her and draw her aside. We sit on the steps.

Her name is Temsutula Imsong—she is thirty-two—born in a village called Ungma in Nagaland. She studied in Shillong, went on to work in Delhi, and in 2012 came to Ghazipur, near Banaras, to join an NGO started by her friend—an ex-Navy man—who is now her husband. That's how she first set eyes on the ghats of Banaras.

'This ghat was an open toilet when I first saw it,' she tells me. 'It was buried under silt—you couldn't see the steps—and people were relieving themselves wherever they pleased.'

A few months ago, she and a woman friend—who has now left Banaras—pooled in money to buy brooms and buckets and masks. With the help of local boatmen and idlers on the ghat, they began cleaning it.

'Were you inspired by the Swachh Bharat campaign?'

'No, it was my idea. But, when we were cleaning up the place, we could hear passersby saying, "Look! Modiji's campaign is on."'

Modi has acknowledged her work. He mentioned her in two tweets, she says. A local newspaper called her '*Kashi ki bahu*'—the daughter-in-law of Kashi. 'That's not correct, I am the daughter-in-law of Ghazipur,' she laughs, 'but I take that as a compliment.'

More boys step forward to touch her feet.

'How long did it take you to clean up the ghat?' I ask her.

'Five days.'

'And how much did it cost you?'

'3,000 rupees.'

13.

WHEN YOU THINK Banaras you hear temple bells and chants or a full-throated rendition of a raga—not quite the place where you would expect a vivacious radio jockey to guide you through the day by playing popular film songs.

'Banaras has not one but four FM stations,' Akanksha, the young RJ who had hosted the event at Prabhu Ghat, tells me when we meet the following afternoon at Assi Ghat. In Banaras, if you are meeting someone, the venue is invariably Assi Ghat.

Akanksha is a minor celebrity in Banaras. Not just her voice, even her face, thanks to Facebook, is familiar to young listeners. I find many regulars at Assi greeting her. It wasn't very long ago when Akanksha would be walking the same ghat as a faceless aspirant.

She tells me, 'I come from Bahraich, have you heard of it? It's a town in Uttar Pradesh, on the border with Nepal.'

'Of course I have.'

'So I was born in Bahraich. My father works in a bank, my mother is a housewife. Once I finished my twelfth standard, in 2007, my parents decided to send me and my younger sister to Banaras for further studies. I had a cousin living in Banaras, near BHU, so finding a place to stay was not a problem.

'The idea was to take admission in BSc, and at the same time attend coaching to prepare for the entrance exams of various engineering colleges. Within days of arriving in Banaras, I was struck by facial paralysis. In a way it was good that the paralysis struck after I reached here because there is a big hospital in BHU. Had it happened back in Bahraich I wouldn't have got immediate care.

'The doctor had no idea why it had happened, but he didn't want any stress on my jaw for the next three to four months, which meant I was not to speak or chew hard or undertake any strenuous activity.

'Those were dark days. The only consolation was that the room which my cousin and his wife had given us to stay in had no mirror, so I didn't get to see how distorted my face had become. But when relatives came to visit, I could see the shock on their faces when they saw me.

'Around this time my sister too was not keeping well. She had a hormonal disorder, and I had to look after her too. On top of it, the cousin's wife was pregnant, which meant I was also expected to do the cooking and cleaning. She was against hiring a maid because she believed the maid would steal.

'When I began to feel better I joined college, even though I was still not speaking unless it was absolutely necessary. And because I was not speaking much, I would spend most of my time observing my classmates, and I soon realised that joining this college was probably the biggest mistake of my life.

'As it is I hated the college for being a girls-only college. I had studied in a co-ed school and I strongly believe that every school and college in this country should be co-ed. On top of that, the girls in my college were so petty and narrow-minded. Even if someone wore jeans, they would pass nasty remarks—can you imagine?

'That is why I made hardly any friends in college. All my friends today are either from my schooldays or people I met after I left college. There was another reason why I did not make friends in college. The younger sister of the cousin's wife also studied in the same college and she would report everything I did. Once I was hanging out with a girl who was a Patel, and when I reached home the cousin's wife—such a nasty woman—asked me how could I, a Rajput, hang out with a girl who was a Patel, apparently a lower caste.

'Until then I was not aware of discrimination on the basis of caste or religion. In Bahraich, nearly 30 per cent of the population was Muslim. Our tailor was a Muslim, our milkman was a Muslim. Many of my classmates were Muslims. We did not differentiate. As for Patels, I had no idea they supposedly belonged to a lower caste. The only Patel I had heard of until then was Amisha Patel'—the actress—'and so when I met my Patel classmate, I was like "Wow, she shares her surname with the actress!"

'But my cousin's wife was always careful to know people's castes—and mind you, she was an educated woman, a law graduate, a product of BHU. Because of her behaviour, because of all the work I had to do at home, because of my ill health, I felt very constricted. There was hardly any time to study. As a result, I scored only 51 per cent in the first year of BSc. That is another reason why I don't have good memories of college.

'But one good thing came out of my going to college: I overcame my fear of the dead. The college was on the other side of Dashashwamedha, so from my home I would take an autorickshaw to Godowlia and from there walk to the college. On the way I would cross Manikarnika, where bodies would be coming in for cremation or already burning. Even from the classroom we could hear funeral processions passing by, chanting: "*Ram naam satya hai*!"

'In Bahraich, we used to be so scared of the concept of death. I remember a time when someone in the neighbourhood had died and we were so scared by the news that we stayed home all day, doors and windows tightly shut. But in Banaras, death became a part of life.

'By the time I finished college, I had given up the idea of becoming an engineer. I began preparing for an MBA and at the same time joined a diploma course in BHU—just for the experience of studying in BHU. It was a course in office management and business communications.

'I had barely finished the course when I got to know about a vacancy in the radio station. I applied for the job. There were four to five rounds of interviews. Luckily for me, the company policy was to prefer someone raw over a trained professional so that they could mould the candidate to their needs. I was selected. This was in 2011.

'For a long time I did not tell my mother I had got the job. I was not sure how she was going to react. She was expecting that I would be an engineer or an MBA. Finally I had to tell her because I had to open a salary account in the bank and I needed certain documents to be sent from home. She was, as I had expected, not at all happy that I had become an RJ. For a long time she did not tell my father about my job.

'But my father, when he eventually learned about it, was happy. My mother too came round. When people would ask her what I was up to and she would reply that I was an RJ, they would react, "*Arrey wah*!" That's when she began to realise that being an RJ was not such a bad thing.'

'Tell me about your first day at work.'

'On the very first day my boss told me that the company, as an afterthought, had decided to hire me as a receptionist but that I could double as an RJ as and when required. My heart sank, then I found out it was a prank. I was asked to buy treats for the entire office. I ordered burgers and pizzas. For almost three months I did nothing except track rival channels. It was a honeymoon period for me. Then the training began.

'For someone coming from Bahraich, the channel was a bit of a culture shock. I think it was my first or second week at work when, one morning, I was standing by the desk of a fellow RJ, a girl from Banaras. When she opened her drawer, I saw a packet of cigarettes inside. I was so shocked that I had to call my sister and tell her what I saw. My sister was like, "Oh my god, she smokes! But she sounds so virtuous while on air."

'Oh yes, there had been another culture shock before that, during the final round of interviews, when the regional director asked me to tell a dirty joke.'

'Did you?'

'Yes, I managed. There are some dirty jokes that degrade women, but there are others that are clean. Mine was a "clean" dirty joke.'

'Let me hear it.'

'Once upon a time, the great musician Tansen was overcome by an irresistible urge to suck the boobs of Emperor Akbar's wife. He approached the royal vizier Birbal, who told him he could arrange for it provided Tansen paid him ten gold coins. Tansen agreed. In the night, Birbal put itching powder in the queen's blouse. The next day, when the queen put on the blouse, her boobs begin to itch unbearably. The emperor was worried, until Birbal came up with a solution. "Your Majesty," he said, "if a man with a melodious voice is allowed to suck Her Majesty's breasts, she will be cured of the itching." Tansen is summoned and his desire is fulfilled, but he promptly forgets about the promise of ten gold coins. Upon which Birbal puts the same powder in the emperor's underwear.'

We burst out laughing. The joke makes Akbar seem remote, even fictional, but he is a real character in the pages of Banaras's history. His reign witnessed its revival as a centre of Hindu pilgrimage after it had been sacked repeatedly by Muslim invaders.

'Do you still live with your cousin and his wife?' I ask Akanksha.

'No way,' she replies, 'we lived there only for a year. After I got poor marks we moved to a paying-guest accommodation where my youngest sister also joined us. We are three sisters—I am the oldest. I now live with the youngest. The one in the middle, who had a hormonal disorder, has now moved to Lucknow for higher studies.'

'How has the radio job changed you?'

'I am very happy that I am a radio jockey—you know why? Had I been working with an MNC, I would have been slogging for the prosperity of someone else, someone who may not have even belonged to India. But radio allows you to reach out to your own people. What you say on air can make a difference to people's lives, and that's very gratifying.

'My outlook towards life has changed altogether. There was a time when I believed—was made to believe— that we are born to make others happy, and felt guilty if I did anything to please only myself. I now see nothing wrong in doing things that make me happy.

'I had many complexes when I came from Bahraich. I am quite short and I don't think I am good-looking, so I always felt inferior to others. A child is born without knowing what is beautiful and what is ugly: it is told what they are. I remember the case of my mother. She too is short and plain-looking, and she was constantly reminded of that fact by my paternal grandmother and other relatives.

'But I have largely overcome that complex now, mainly because of my listeners. They first liked my voice and later, when I started a Facebook page, they started liking my pictures too. I have got some 11,000 followers on Facebook, that's a big number for a place like Banaras. When so many people start telling you that you look nice, you tend to think, "Okay, maybe I *am* nice-looking."

'I am more confident now. That's largely because of my boss. He is never lenient with me simply because I am a woman. If I am caught up at work till late in the night, he will never say, "It's getting late, you better go home." If work has to be done, it has to be done, no matter how late.'

'How has Banaras changed you?'

'*Banaras ne mujhe seekhna sikhaya*'—Banaras taught me that one must keep learning—'It may be a small town but is very cultured and progressive. Women bathe in the ghats here but you won't find anyone standing and staring at them. Even some of the boatmen will know a raga or two because they all sit through concerts. Even the least educated of the lot are capable of holding a meaningful conversation. All this inspires you to learn new things. Even I am going to take singing lessons from tomorrow.'

'Why singing?'

'Sometimes singers on my show ask me to sing along. But I can't sing to save my life, I only hum. So I thought, why not learn singing?'

'Who are you going to learn from?'

'There is a didi who lives very close to Assi. She belongs to some place near Patna. She studies in BHU. She too lives in a paying-guest accommodation.'

'Can I meet her sometime?'

'Sure, I will arrange a meeting. So, as I was saying, *Banaras ne mujhe seekhna sikhaya*. I also intend to learn playing the guitar. When you learn something new, you go back to being a student, you feel young all over again. If you live in Banaras, you stay young forever.'

14.

LUCK IS ON my side. Just when Akanksha and I are preparing to leave Assi, we bump into the didi, the music teacher. And the didi, who I had imagined to be stern and much older than Akanksha, turns out to be a young woman herself, her features so striking that she would stand out in any crowd. Her name is Surabhi. She hails from Danapur in Bihar and has been living in Banaras for over three years now. The first thing I notice about her is her bright lipstick.

I ask the two ladies to join me for dinner at Pizzeria. Over rotis and daal and paneer butter masala, we make small talk. Akanksha is bubbly, but Surabhi is a little shy in my presence.

The conversation drifts from classical music to life in Banaras to the idea of having pure and simple fun. For them, I gather, the very fact that they are living alone in Banaras is fun. Not so much because of the things they can do, but because of the things they don't have to do, such as answering queries about their whereabouts to their parents, enduring the taunts of critical relatives, avoiding the prying eyes of neighbours. Life isn't easy for young, single women in a small town in the Hindi heartland. Their actions are invariably guided by the second-biggest worry afflicting Indians (the first being the lack of money): what will people say?

'The other night,' Surabhi is finally opening up, 'five of us—five girls on three scooters—roamed the streets of Banaras all night. Every now and then we would stop for chaat, for paan, for chai. Such fun! We got back home only at five in the morning.'

She is animatedly recalling an activity so innocent that I don't have the heart to ask if her idea of fun includes meeting guys or drinking alcohol. Akanksha decides to leave immediately after dinner: her sister is waiting at home. I walk Surabhi out of the restaurant.

'Where do you live?' I ask her.

'Just a five-minute walk away.'

'Should I walk you home?'

'I am not in a hurry to get home.'

The ghat is lit up but the river is black. We sit on the steps, gazing at the nothingness. We sit in silence, but the silence isn't awkward; it feels as if I've known Surabhi for a long time. She is now humming a tune.

'Why don't you sing?' I ask her.

'Don't blame me if I bore you.'

'I won't.'

She sings a portion of an Asha Bhosle song I've grown up listening to: *Dil cheez kya hai aap meri jaan lijiye.* Then another song, then another, until I realise it is close to midnight. I have a long walk ahead. Maybe I will find a cycle-rickshaw, but the gate of the lodge will be shut and I will have to keep banging on it until someone inside wakes up and opens the latch.

As we walk towards the main road, she is humming a song that I recognise instantly: *Aaj jaane ki zidd na karo.*

'I would like to know more about you,' I tell her.

'Why don't we meet tomorrow?'
'Where do we meet?'
'Right here.'
'What time?'
'At sunrise?'

15.

THE ASCENT OF the sun has lit up the sandstone structures that define Banaras. I have begun my walk in the direction of Assi Ghat.

To understand what people mean when they say time flies, you only have to look at the rising or setting sun and then look away for a few moments. When you return your gaze to the sun, you will find it to have moved several notches higher in the sky—that's the flight of time.

Banaras, however, remains untouched by time. Invaders came and went, rulers changed, the earth went around the sun a few thousand times, but this riverside settlement has remained the one-stop shop for seekers of salvation longer than time.

I am thinking of Surabhi. Is she, by any chance, going to determine how I spend my remaining days in Banaras? I have only a few days left before I return, and Banaras is beginning to get interesting. I have seen nearly all that there is to see for a visitor, idled away my time on the ghats, rubbed shoulders with sadhus and pilgrims, drunk tea with the locals, but how well do I know Banaras? I hardly do. Maybe that man with a Canadian wife was right: it can take many lifetimes to understand Banaras. If that is the case, the multitude that comes to Banaras seeking moksha never quite gets to understand Banaras because they get freed from the cycle of rebirths before they can do so.

I am at Tulsi Ghat when Surabhi calls to say she will be late. To kill time I climb up the ghat into the old building where Tulsidas, the sixteenth-century poet and saint, is believed to have lived. I bow before the idol of Hanuman and read the *Hanuman Chalisa* inscribed on a stone slab just to see how much of it I remember. I realise that with a bit of prompting here and there, I can still recite the forty verses without looking at the text.

I climb up the building into the room where, in a grilled enclosure, is Tulsidas's cot with his framed portrait above it. In the portrait Tulsidas is depicted as bearded, being fanned with a whisk by an attendant. A contemporary of William Shakespeare, he is considered one of the greatest poets ever, if not the greatest. In the Hindi heartland they say poetry did not make Tulsidas, but it was Tulsidas who performed a great service to the art. It is a different matter that during his lifetime he was hounded by Brahmins for compromising on the sanctity of the *Ramayana*—originally composed in Sanskrit—by retelling it in Awadhi, the local language.

The two windows of this sunbathed room offer a majestic view of the sun climbing above the river. Tulsidas must have woken up to the same spectacle every morning—if only one were sure that he actually lived in this building. Tulsidas died in 1630, and it is very unlikely that a humble dwelling from that time would still be standing.

But such details shouldn't matter. Tulsidas was a true-blue Banarasi and he certainly lived somewhere here if not exactly here, because it is widely accepted that he died at Assi Ghat. Back in his time, this spot would have come under the jurisdiction of Assi Ghat, which is barely a few paces away and where Surabhi is waiting for me now.

16.

'I AM VERY afraid of water,' says Surabhi.

'Nothing to fear,' assures the boatman, who has overheard her.

We are on water, coloured by the reflection of the sunlit riverside buildings. How quickly the perspective changes! Until a moment ago, Surabhi and I were two extras in a movie called Banaras, and now, from the boat, it feels as if we are watching the same movie sitting in a theatre.

We are going from Assi to Dashashwamedha. That's the plan for now.

'So tell me, how did you land up in Banaras?' I ask Surabhi.

'Back home, I had done my BA in music. My teacher suggested I come to Banaras for a master's degree in music from the BHU, that's how I came here.'

'Was it easy to get admission?'

'Far from it. I had to first clear a written test. Then there was to be a practical exam. I was a little anxious, also because there were only six seats in the general category. I knew I had to perform well. So I looked around for a guru.

'I finally found a place where they taught vocals. But I left after three classes because I realised the teachers were themselves research students, and had nothing new to teach me. On top of that, they were charging 400 rupees per hour—a bit too much.

'Then a teacher at BHU advised me to listen to Kishori Amonkar and adopt her style. I began listening to Kishori Amonkar on CD. I was listening to her day and night, even though at the time I had trouble with my right ear. The ear would hurt even more when I spoke. It was so painful that I would cry. So I would plug the earphone to the left ear and listen to her.

'I was not happy with the way I was singing, but those who heard me said I was doing fine. I prepared myself with three ragas—Purya Dhanashri, Miyan Malhar and Ramkali—and finally, on the day of the practicals, decided to sing Purya Dhanashri.

'The practical exam began at nine in the morning, and my turn came at four in the afternoon. When I went in I was nervous, but as I started singing, it all came to me. When I walked out, I could hear people asking, "Who sang just now?" I stood second.

'But life wasn't easy once I settled down. Relatives were constantly visiting Banaras and they would invite themselves to stay in my flat. I would have to cook for them, give them tea whenever they asked for it, wash the utensils.

'Once, a distant relative suffering from cancer came to Banaras for treatment at BHU. Naturally, he stayed with me—not just him, but also three other people who had accompanied him. I hardly knew those people, but I would make breakfast for them, go to college, come back to prepare lunch for them, find some time to practise singing, make dinner for them, wash the utensils, wash their clothes. This went on for three months. I was working like an ox.'

Her eyes brim with tears and she looks away. I too look away. I see a bunch of pilgrims from Maharashtra, waist-deep in water, appearing to greet me with their hands folded and raised—they are actually saluting the sun. I guess they are from Maharashtra from the turbans worn by their companions who've finished bathing. The boat is a good place to gauge the diversity of India: pilgrims come from every corner, bringing along their colours and distinct mannerisms. In Banaras, the much worn-out expression—colours of India—rings real.

'You continue to live in the same flat?' I ask Surabhi.

'No, I moved out. That's another story.'

'What's that?'

'During the monsoon of 2013, barely a year after I moved here, Banaras was flooded. My mother and brother were visiting me at the time. Initially we didn't realise the severity of the situation. First, the power went off. There was no power for two days. Then the water came into our street. My landlord said this happened every year and there was nothing to worry about. But my mother thought we should stock up on food, so she sent my brother to pick up some groceries.

'When my brother left for the market, the water was ankle-deep, but by the time he returned, it was up to his knees. Now my landlord began to panic. He lived on the ground floor and we lived on the one above it. He began moving his belongings into our house. In a matter of a few hours the water was waist-deep.

'We knew we had no option but to leave right away. We had a relative who lived at a safe distance from the riverside. I quickly packed my certificates and important documents. The water was up to my chest when we left. I was crying as we waded through the water. I told you I am scared of water.

'We must have waded for only about a kilometre or so, but when you are moving through chest-deep water, it seems like a never-ending trek. I even spotted snakes swimming about me. Each time I saw a snake I wanted to run, but how does one run through water?

'We somehow made it to the main road, where we managed to find an autorickshaw to the relative's house. A few days later, when I returned to the flat to collect the rest of my belongings, I found my scooter lying by a shop on the road. It had been washed away but, thankfully for me, did not go too far.

'We stayed in the relative's house for about two weeks. With their help we found another flat, where I lived for only nine months because the landlord was a very interfering sort. Eventually, I moved to a paying-guest accommodation. That's where I live now. The problem with staying in a flat was that I had people constantly coming over to stay. I hardly had any time and space for riyaaz (practice). Now that I have enrolled for MPhil, riyaaz is very important for me.

'Life is still not easy. I am on my toes all day. I go for a walk in the morning, do puja for half-an-hour, cook and eat breakfast, rush to college, return home to have lunch, do riyaaz, go out to teach my students—I need to teach in order to grow as a professional. But yes, now there is no one to tell me what I can do or what I cannot do. I can do my own thing.'

Once we get off the boat at Dashashwamedha, Surabhi suggests we visit the Vishwanath Temple. She hasn't been to the temple in a while, and now is a good time to go there because she hasn't eaten yet. God must be worshipped, ideally, on an empty stomach. But the queue at the temple is so long that she is intimidated and disappointed at once.

'I'll take you to another Shiva temple,' I tell her.

'Really? Which one?'

'Come with me. I am sure you've never been there before.'

We walk back to the river and then walk from one ghat to another in the direction of Manikarnika. As we happen to pass a newly-wed couple taking pictures, I ask Surabhi if her parents have started pestering her to get married.

'The search for a boy has been on for a while, just that they haven't found anyone suitable yet,' she says.

'What kind of a boy would be suitable for you?'

'He should have a decent job, and be ideally from the same caste. I am not very particular about caste, but my parents are.'

'In other words you don't have a boyfriend.'

'I don't. I never had the courage to find one.'

'Not even in Banaras? You've been living alone here.'

'No one interesting enough. Had I found someone interesting, I would have found the courage as well.'

'Please invite me to your wedding.'

'Sure, *bilkul*! You know something, my father can read palms, and he says I have seven marriages written on my palm.'

'*Seven*?'

'Yes, seven.'

'Do you believe him?'

'I don't know whether to believe him or not.'

We arrive at Lalita Ghat. The piles of wood at the neighbouring Manikarnika come into view. I lead her up the steps to the Nepali Temple, which is open but deserted. Surabhi covers her head as she enters the sanctum sanctorum and shuts her eyes to pray. I am curious to know what she is praying for but I think I have an idea.

When we step out of the sanctum sanctorum we are greeted by a young, cheerful Nepali man, who turns out to be the caretaker.

'Have you been to Nepal?' he asks us.

'No,' I reply, 'not yet.'

'Have you heard of the Pashupatinath Temple in Kathmandu?'

'Of course I have.'

'This temple is a replica of that. Very old temple, this one, built by the Rana some 200 years ago. How long have the two of you been married?'

Surabhi and I look at each other. She is suppressing a giggle. I tell the man, 'We have just married. We have come to Banaras on a holiday.'

'I should have known. Please come with me.'

He leads us into what seems to be the temple office. He pulls out a rolled-up poster from a shelf and respectfully hands it over to us: 'This is my wedding gift. May Pashupatinath bless you both!'

It turns out to be a picture of the Pashupatinath Temple, which the Shiva fan in me resolves to visit some day.

'Now it's my turn to take you somewhere,' Surabhi tells me as we descend the steep steps.

'Where?'

'To the Kala Bhairava Temple. They say if you are taking up a new assignment or starting a new job or project, you must take the blessings of Kala Bhairava.'

'Before that let me show you Manikarnika. Been there before?'

'Never.'

As we walk in the direction of the piles of wood and burning pyres, a bunch of buffaloes emerges from the river and, in an orderly fashion, climbs up the steps of Manikarnika and disappears into its lanes. Buffaloes are a common sight in Banaras, but their presence at Manikarnika serves as a reminder that the buffalo happens to be the mount of Yama, the god of death.

Surabhi is calm at the sight of burning pyres. I tell her that I had cremated my mother at this ghat. I am not sure whether she has heard me: she is lost in thought, her gaze fixed on something far away.

17.

MANY YEARS AGO, when I used to work with a newspaper in Delhi, a young female colleague said to me one evening: 'Every Bengali man is Jesus Christ, do you know why?'

'Why?'

'Because he thinks his mother is a virgin, and the mother thinks her son is God.'

The joke has stayed with me, not without reason. While I was not foolish enough to believe that my mother was a virgin—except for a brief period when I thought I had been purchased from the hospital for 105 rupees (the hospital bill had remained preserved for a long time)—my mother certainly regarded me as a child personally hand-delivered to her by God. The child—who remained a child for her even after he had hair sprouting from his upper lip—was meant to be protected from all kinds of potential harm, including the inauspiciousness of death. I was asked to stay clear of any home where a dead body lay and was not supposed to touch members of that family or mourners who had visited that home. Even if a parent of a friend died, I was to keep a distance from the body. She saw death as a contagious disease, little realising that every child contracts the disease the moment it is born.

My mother had another concern: what if I abandoned her once she became old? She would, from time to time, remind me that a man, no matter how prosperous he gets, always remains indebted to his mother because no amount of money can repay what one owes his mother. To support her case, she would tell me the story of a temple in Banaras. She had heard the story from her maternal grandmother, who spent most of her life in Banaras.

According to the story, a rich man once built a temple in Banaras in his mother's honour. Once the temple was ready, he brought the mother to the spot to show it off. 'This,' he proudly declared to her, 'repays everything I owe you!' He had barely uttered these words when a foundation stone sank deeper into the soil and the temple began to lean.

The leaning temple is a reality. The story behind it is just that—a story—even though the temple, called Ratneshwar Mahadev temple and said to be built in the 1820s, is also often referred to as Matri Rin—Mother's Debt—temple. It stands, of all places, at the Manikarnika, in the river, the sanctum sanctorum under water most of the time.

The temple had been in my line of vision when I touched fire to my mother's lips all those years ago. She had been spared what she feared: neglect in old age. She didn't even live to be sixty. If she had lived three days longer she would have been fifty-nine. In death she exposed me to the contagious disease she had sought to protect me from all her life: there were bodies all around me and I was a mourner myself. How would I have felt then if I found someone not wanting to touch me because I was inauspicious?

Now, as Surabhi and I survey the Manikarnika, I realise that this temple with a faulty foundation was one of the foundation stones of my life. The stone slipped away with my mother's death, setting me free.

18.

BEFORE THE LAST rites of my mother, I had come to Banaras on three occasions.

At the age of seventeen, after I wrote—and cleared—my first competitive exam, the written test for the National Defence Academy, I had been called by the Air Force Selection Board at Varanasi. I stayed on the campus for five days—my first ever stay away from home—along with about forty other candidates from across India, undergoing a number of tests that would decide whether we were good enough to join the Air Force.

The tests would end by noon, and we would have almost the entire day to ourselves. The candidates were all in their late teens, and each enjoyed the freedom of being away from home. We roamed the streets of Banaras, watched movies; the more adventurous ones smoked and stared at girls. I hadn't started smoking yet, and I still don't stare. I derived pleasure in quietly breaking away from the others and slipping into the railway station to have a dosa. While the dosa was being prepared, I would have two idlis.

At the end of the five days, a majority of the candidates, including myself, stood rejected. We had been found lacking in OLQ: officer-like qualities. I took the train back home to Kanpur.

Then, at the age of twenty-three, when I was into my first job—as a sub-editor with the *Pioneer* newspaper, which had just been launched in Kanpur—I found myself in the cricket team of Kanpur journalists that was headed for a tournament in Banaras.

We took the train from Kanpur sometime in the afternoon, and I couldn't enjoy the first few hours of the journey because I was troubled by a speck of dust that had gotten into my eye. Finally a fellow journalist—a reporter from a Hindi paper—manipulated my eyelid with his fingers and the speck miraculously disappeared. I now looked out of the window: the magical hour of dusk had descended on the rustic landscape of eastern Uttar Pradesh. The senior-most journalist in the group pulled out a bottle of whisky from his bag. I hadn't taken to alcohol yet, but I did have a drink.

We reached Banaras later that evening and checked into a dharmashala. When I woke up the next morning, I found half the team standing in a huddle against the grille of the balcony. They were peering into the terrace of a neighbouring house, where a young woman sat on her haunches grinding spices on a slab of stone.

The woman wore a sari—but no blouse—and one of her breasts was bared, swinging to the rhythm of her arms that were meticulously grinding the spices into a paste. She was aware of the gaze of the strangers but didn't seem to care.

We lost the match that morning, against journalists from Lucknow, and were out of the tournament. After a sumptuous post-match lunch, while the rest of the Kanpur team decided to nap, a teammate and I decided to look around Banaras.

We went to the Vishwanath Temple and then to Dashashwamedha, where a large crowd had gathered to watch the shooting of a Hindi film, *Ghatak*. At a distance, I could see the actor Sunny Deol, standing waist-deep in the river. The scene was about the hero immersing the ashes of a loved one in the Ganga.

The sun was setting when we left the ghat and walked back into the galis of Banaras. I soon noticed a woman following us and told my companion about it. 'Yes, she has been following us for some time now,' he said.

'But why is she following us?'

'She is a prostitute,' he whispered. 'She can tell we are outsiders.'

It was suddenly thrilling, at least to me, that we were being followed by a woman. I had never encountered a prostitute before.

We entered a sweetshop, sat at a table and ordered lassi. The woman came behind us and sat at the next table. She looked at us intently, perhaps waiting for us to initiate the deal. But we were drained of all courage, even though we had been excited a few minutes before.

'Are you looking for something?' she finally asked us.

My companion and I looked at each other and he said to me, 'Please tell her to go away.' I told him, 'Why don't you tell her?' But neither of us looked in her direction. The lassi arrived and the woman left.

The next morning, the team took a bus to Mughal Sarai, a big railway junction barely ten kilometres away, where it was far easier to find a train to Kanpur than from Banaras.

Then Banaras was forgotten—for a while.

In 2007, when I began working on *Chai, Chai*, which was about life in small towns that serve as large railway junctions, I returned to Mughal Sarai. I had, by then, completely forgotten that Banaras lay very close to it.

I was reminded of the proximity only when I heard taxi drivers calling out to passengers emerging from the Mughal Sarai station: 'Banaras! Banaras! Banaras!' But I had no intention of making a trip. I had only four days in Mughal Sarai and I was anxious to make the most of them.

But one morning, as I walked past the drivers chanting the name of Banaras, I thought, why not? I found myself drawn by the name. There is a halo around it.

I hired a taxi. The driver, I found out later, was too young to have a license. He drove the worn-out Ambassador, nevertheless, at great speed. The rear-view mirrors of the cab were missing. Only the horn seemed to be in perfect working condition. I was greatly relieved when we finally approached the river and the ghats of Banaras came into view.

Banaras now looked different to me. I was struck by its timelessness. Under the parasols that give the riverside of Banaras its distinct look sat priests guiding pilgrims through rituals that mark the different stages of life, right from birth to death and everything in between. In India, faith in rituals often outweighs faith in God. Rituals keep Banaras alive.

I spent five hours in Banaras, with the young taxi driver acting as my guide, and saw far more than I had during my previous visits. I visited the temple that had given me my name; I walked through the labyrinth of alleys; I took a boat ride. I also saw something else, which I recorded in my notebook after returning to my lodge in Mughal Sarai:

'I lost count of the funeral processions that were coming in: some processions celebrated the deliverance of their dead with drum beats and dancing; the others glumly chanted, "*Ram naam satya hai*!" It was like witnessing a carnival of the dead, with each procession showcasing its bier and the dead joyfully raising invisible thumbs from under their shrouds to exclaim, "We made it! We made it to Banaras!"

'The images of the bedecked biers kept swimming in my head as the Ambassador rattled down the dusty road to Mughal Sarai. Everybody has to die one day, but you don't want to be reminded of that, do you? It is, however, not the thought of your own death that makes the sight of the biers so terrifying: it is actually the thought of your near and dear ones being carried away in that fashion. It is a thought you consider secretly in the deepest crevices of your heart, not even sharing it aloud with your own self.'

I incorporated these lines, along with a brief description of my visit to Banaras, in the book, which I finished writing over the next eighteen months. The book was still with the printer, set to roll off the press any moment, when I was back on the streets of Banaras, lending a shoulder to the string-cot that carried my mother's body.

I am back again now.

19.

'SO SIX MORE marriages to go for you,' I tell Surabhi.

'What do you mean?'

'Why, one just got ticked off the list.'

'Oh that!' she laughs. 'I wonder what made him think we were a couple.'

After a quick visit to the Kala Bhairava Temple, which was so crowded that I had a hand on my hip pocket all along to protect my wallet, we are now back in the alleys, looking for a place to have breakfast. I have a place in mind, Kachoriwali Gali, where shops supposedly sell the best kachoris in all of Banaras, only I am not sure where it is. Surabhi hasn't even heard of the place.

I ask for directions, but we find ourselves being shunted from one alley to another without success. It is quite likely that its existence is apocryphal, but since I am in agreeable company, I'm using this opportunity to lose myself in the galis of Banaras once more. They are so narrow that they can barely hold five adults shoulder to shoulder, but they cradle a culture whose reputation has reached round the world. They are the arteries of Banaras, lodged between two parallel curves: the riverbank and the main road.

Do I find Banaras here? I am not going to risk making such a tall claim. But I do see a living settlement that came into existence at a time when human feet were the only mode of transport and fire the sole source of light. Babylon perished, but Banaras has survived. And unlike the nearby ancient settlement of Prayag, which became Allahabad under the Mughals, Banaras even retained its various ancient names (in spite of being once rechristened Muhammadabad by Aurangzeb). Banaras, like its ruler Shiva, has transcended time and space.

The search for kachoris finally brings us to Vishwanath Gali, where I ask a paan-seller for directions. 'Kachoriwali Gali now exists only in name,' he informs me. 'Only one or two shops on it remain. But why do you want to go there?'

'Why, to eat kachoris.'

'Why would you want to eat there? *Murda phoonk kar log wahaan khaane aate hain*'—People go to eat there after burning bodies.

Murda phoonkna is a crude way to describe cremation, and that kills my appetite for kachoris. We resume our walk and finally stop at a sweetshop where puris are being freshly fried.

'What next?' Surabhi asks me after we have eaten.

'You tell me.'

'No, you tell me.'

20.

SURABHI AND I take a boat back to Assi, where we climb the steps to Pizzeria to have coffee. A sweet scent of incense wafts out of the Kashi Annapurna Book House next door. A part of me is tempted to walk in. Very few places on earth are as comforting as a bookshop, and the rate at which their number is shrinking accords a special charm to those still standing. And this is a bookshop with a view.

Yet another part of me resists walking in because each time I am inside I feel like an ant, prone to be stamped out by the tomes on its shelves. There are people who've spent a significant part of their lives researching Banaras, whereas I am merely a wanderer claiming familiarity with the city just because it was the birthplace of his name and the place his mother chose to die in.

My familiarity with this bookshop, however, is real. I know its story.

Once upon a time, in the town of Rae Bareli, lived a boy who was married off, against his wishes, at the age of sixteen. He abandoned his home—and his bride—and came to Banaras to become a sadhu. He found a guru and took the name of Kashi Ashram and went on to build a small ashram at Assi.

Twenty years later, Annapurna, the girl he was married to, also arrived in Banaras in search of him.

They happened to meet one morning at the ghat when he had gone there to bathe. She fell at his feet and asked him why he had abandoned her. He took her to his guru, who advised him to let her be with him. But Kashi Ashram disagreed with his guru and instead rented a house for the woman.

Over time, Annapurna too moved into the ashram and led a pious life. In her family there was a boy, barely five, whose mother had died and whose father had remarried. She brought the boy, Kamalkant, to Banaras and raised him. Kamalkant, when he grew up, took up a job in a pharmacy and then tried his hand in the tea business before devoting himself fulltime to helping Kashi Ashram in discharging his religious duties.

By now Kashi Ashram had begun giving public discourses on a piece of land right outside the ashram. His discourses became so popular that the king of Banaras decided to donate that land to him. When Kashi Ashram died in 1995, Kamalkant, by then married and the father of two sons, inherited the place.

In 2003, Kamalkant's two sons, Manish and Akash, began to utilise the space where Kashi Ashram gave his discourses to sell books. The books would be laid out on old tables. So good was the response to the makeshift bookshop that within two years, they built a proper shop on its proceeds, complete with glass panels, and named it after Kashi Ashram and his wife. Their uncle, who ran a publishing house called Pilgrims Publishing, gave the boys books worth 30,000 rupees to stock in the new shop.

The story was told to me recently by Akash, now twenty-six, who said the business remains so *zabardast*—tremendous—that sometimes the brothers miss lunch because there are far too many customers to attend to. While the bookshop is their source of livelihood, their life revolves around the Shiva temple inside their house.

Every morning, they spend two hours cleaning and decorating the shrine; no one in the family eats anything before food is offered to God; and aarti must be conducted every evening, rain or shine. Even when the family had to move out during the recent floods—the one that had displaced Surabhi as well—the two brothers would wade into their home every evening to hold the aarti in knee-deep water, often in the company of a snake or two. Their father still bathes in the Ganga every morning without fail, though the sons prefer to bathe at home because they find the river too polluted for daily dips.

I finally step into the shop. Akash is happy to see me. 'Have you read *Kashi ka Assi*?' he asks.

'No, but I have been wanting to. Do you have a copy?'

'Yes, only one copy left.'

'Great. I've seen the trailer of *Mohalla Assi* though.'

Mohalla Assi is a Bollywood film based on *Kashi ka Assi*, a collection of stories by the famous Banaras-based writer Kashinath Singh. Its release in the theatres has been stayed by the court because some self-righteous elements were offended by the trailer, which shows the characters, including a man in the garb of Lord Shiva, frequently mouthing the profanity '*bhosrikay*'.

I buy the copy and, with Surabhi by my side, climb down to the ghat and occupy a bench. To get my eyes acclimatised to the Hindi script—it's been years since I read anything in Hindi—I read the first page slowly and aloud. Kashinath Singh declares in the very first sentence that his book isn't intended for kids and the elderly or for those who don't realise that the relationship between

Assi and polite language is akin to the one shared by two battling sisters-in-law.

Having thus prepared the reader for what to expect, he informs you that '*Har Har Mahadev*' and '*bhosrikay*' are the two most common greetings in Banaras: while the first needs to be said with some force, the second rolls off the tongue easily.

Then he proceeds to define the quintessential Banarasi in a single sentence: '*Zamaane ko laude par rakh kar masti se ghoomne ki mudra* identity card *hai iska*'—one who struts about in a carefree fashion, with the world placed on his dick (essentially, one who doesn't give a fuck).

Surabhi is in splits as I read. She punches my arm: 'You are so bad! Read it when I am not around.'

'You must be quite used to bad words.'

'You can't walk two steps in Banaras without such words reaching your ears. But I find it funny when they come from your mouth.'

'I would like to meet him someday.'

'Who?'

'Kashinath Singh.'

Later that night I stay glued to *Kashi ka Assi*. I don't exactly finish reading it cover to cover but I get the essence. From its pages drips the juice that is Banaras. The multitude that descends on Banaras every day returns home without tasting a drop of it. They get off their bus or train, head for Dashashwamedha, bathe in the river, perform rituals at the ghat, visit the Vishwanath Temple, and find their way back to the bus or railway station.

They carry back a bit of Banaras in the form of Ganga water, but not its essence.

Assi is barely two kilometres south of Dashashwamedha. It is peopled not by pilgrims but by Banarasis. Here you find the juice, imbibed mostly in the form of tea at one of its busy teashops. Between the first and the last sip you get a fair idea of what's going on—in people's lives, in the neighbourhood, in the country. If you keep returning to the teashop, you forge bonds and form associations and before long become a member of the parliament that convenes on rickety benches but wields sufficient power to alter the lives of people in the neighbourhood.

Kashinath Singh made himself a fly on the wall in one such teashop—in fact the most popular teashop in Assi, run by a man called Pappu—and wove laughter-inducing stories that hold a mirror to the people of Assi, their portraits painted in the lingo most familiar to them. Even though he has, quite understandably, passed his work off as fiction, anyone who has walked the galis of Banaras with eyes and ears open can tell the stories are very real—just as real as his definition of a Banarasi.

To me, *Kashi ka Assi* is the most authentic portrait of present-day Banaras—the Banaras that belongs to people and not gods.

21.

TOMORROW EVENING I leave Banaras. I'll be back again, no idea when.

Some people will tell me that I can return only if—and when—Lord Shiva or Ganesha allows me to. There are others who will say that all I would need to do is take the next plane or train in order to be back in their midst.

My heart is heavy at the thought of saying goodbye, and right now I want to soak in the sunrise. I can watch the sun rise back home in Chennai as well, but that would entail waking up early enough and driving to the beach. Not like in Banaras, where I just have to step out of the lodge and walk a few steps. Moreover, the sun appears remote when viewed across the sea. In Banaras, the ascending orange ball is part of the setting, as if hired to give an exclusive performance to the city every morning.

At the Suryodaya Haveli Ghat, a group of Tamil pilgrims are repeating the mantras chanted by a priest, also a Tamil. Further down, at the Chet Singh Ghat, a lone old man is seated in the lotus pose, his hands raised in salutation to the sun. I walk on. On the marhi at the Jain Ghat, a priest seated cross-legged is offering water to the sun in an outstretched palm; right next to him is a man who is still fast asleep, his arms stretched above his head. The two men are blind to the other's existence: one is yet to wake up and the other considers himself awakened, but the marhi belongs to both at the moment.

Further down, at Tulsi Ghat, about a dozen men are standing in single file facing a priest. They are all knee-deep in the river. The men, wearing nothing but white dhotis, have formed a human train: each has an arm placed on the shoulder of the one ahead of him, so that each time the priest blesses the man in the front, the others get blessed too by virtue of touch. These men are doing tarpan, a ritual performed this time of the year to propitiate the spirits of departed ancestors. Since one-to-one sessions would be too time-consuming for the priest and even more expensive for each individual, this ritual is mostly conducted en masse. Each man has a different story and different ancestry, but right now they are collectively reaching out to their respective ancestors through a priest who is guiding them through the rituals mechanically.

I climb up the steps to Tulsidas's house. A long-haired priest at the shrine of Hanuman beckons me. He pours holy water in my palm for me to sip in perfunctory fashion, and then shows me a small broken piece of wood, supposedly from the prow of Tulsidas's personal boat.

'Did he really live in this building?' I ask him.

'Very much so,' he states with conviction. 'Have you been to the akhara set up by him?'

'No.'

'Go take a look. It's located right behind this house.'

Since there is no direct passage from the shrine to the akhara, I climb down and climb up again to reach an alley behind the building to find an open-air gymnasium, complete with a wrestling pit. That's what an akhara means: a traditional gym. Maces and plates and dumbbells are strewn around, but there is not a soul in sight except a middle-aged man who, wearing nothing but a langoti, is lolling in the wrestling pit. To cut short the awkward moments that follow when our eyes meet, he explains: 'I am waiting for my skin to absorb the mud. It's very good for the health.'

'Don't people come here to wrestle?'

'They have left for the day. That's when I come, when everybody has left, so that I can roll in the mud and rub it on my skin. This mud has medicinal properties. Your skin will stay healthy after a mudbath like this. After that, I will bathe in the river, and then, all tension will leave me!'

'How long since you've been coming here?'

'I am forty-five now, and I have been coming here from the age of fifteen. You can calculate from that. Earlier, I would wrestle and do weights, but now I come here only to apply the mud on myself.'

The man gives me his name, Ram Lal. He is a resident of Durgakund, near Assi, and runs a shop that sells items required for rituals. After bathing in the river he visits, without fail, the temples in the neighbourhood and also the Sankat Mochan Temple. That is the city's best-known Hanuman temple, built, not very far from Assi, by Tulsidas during his lifetime. But he doesn't visit the Vishwanath Temple very often because he finds the whole process—depositing valuables, standing in long queues, being frisked—too tedious.

'You never thought of looking for a job outside Banaras?' I ask him.

'That was out of the question,' he says emphatically. '*Ek baar jisko Banaras ka anand mil gaya woh kabhi Banaras chhod kar nahin ja sakta*'—Once you discover the joy of living in Banaras you can never think of leaving.

I am instantly reminded of a line from *Kashi ka Assi*: *Jo mazaa Banaras mein; na Paris mein na Faras mein*—the joy that Banaras offers can be found neither in Paris nor in Persia.

22.

WHILE HAVING BREAKFAST on the terrace of the lodge I find the next table occupied by an elderly couple. The man regards me with caution but the woman has a conversation-inviting smile on her face. They are from Israel.

'Your first visit to India?' I ask them.

'Third, but first time in Varanasi,' she replies.

'What do you like about Varanasi?'

'Oh, I can't even begin to tell you. People here are so happy. They have nothing but still they are happy. Even a child who has no slippers is happy. Not like in our country, where they run after luxury.'

The husband looks away.

'What's written there?' I point to her silver bracelet which has an engraving in Hebrew.

'It says love your neighbour.'

She has probably detected the sarcasm in my smile, because she quickly adds: 'I wish our politicians realised that.'

I have an unfinished task before I leave Banaras. I have spent considerable time at Assi, but I am yet to set foot in Rajghat, at the opposite end of the chain of ghats that make up Banaras. The other day I had set out in its direction but aborted my trek at Prahlad Ghat because it was getting dark and I hadn't found the stretch hospitable enough to keep walking on. Now is a good time to go there, I decide, preferably on a boat because my feet are tired.

I hire a motorised boat—for 1,000 rupees—at Dashashwamedha and set out for Rajghat. Once the boat crosses Manikarnika, the aura of the riverfront begins to diminish. What I am gazing at are ghats too—each has a name and its share of marhis—but nary a tourist or pilgrim. Most of them have clusters of human settlement in the background.

Rajghat, I discover, is just a single ghat away from Prahlad Ghat, where I had terminated my walk the other evening. Had I walked another 100 metres, I would have not only accomplished the feat of walking from one extremity of the riverfront to another but also saved the 1,000 rupees I have just shelled out.

What catches my eye, as soon as I hop off the boat at Rajghat, is a tilted motor launch lodged in the soil. It looks as if it had been washed ashore many moons ago—perhaps during a flood—and has remained that way ever since, considering every inch of it is rusted. The cadaver of this once-beautiful vessel marks the end of the chain of ghats that defines Banaras.

There is a sprinkling of bathers here. The women who've already bathed have spread out their colourful saris on the steps. Towering over the steps is a white temple—a modern construction—built in honour of the fourteenth-century-born mystic poet Saint Ravidas, who was from Banaras.

I climb up the steps and wander around. Under a tree is seated a policeman keeping an eye on the transport of wood. Logs are offloaded here by trucks and carried, by boat, to Manikarnika. A body arrives, tied to the roof of a jeep. It is untied by relatives and carried down the steps to a waiting boat that will take it to Manikarnika. Under another tree, not far away, a just-married couple is putting sweets into each other's mouths while the families cheer.

Tree: man's most loyal friend! It gives you life when alive and in death becomes the pyre so that together you can burn into ash. Now I can see why the poet-saint Kabir, another Banarasi, wrote these lines:

Dekh tamasha lakdi ka
jeete lakdi
marte lakdi.

Behold the spectacle of wood
wood when you're alive
wood when you're dead.

I have read as a child that when Kabir died, an argument broke out between Hindus and Muslims over whether he should be cremated or buried. As they quarrelled, his mortal remains vanished and what remained under the shroud was a mound of flowers. Half those flowers were cremated and the remaining buried.

This, of course, is a story. Today I wonder how it made it to a school textbook. What is true, however, is that Kabir did not die in Banaras. He spent his final days in a place called Maghar, some 200 kilometres north of the city. He chose to do so because Maghar was considered a bad place to die—it was said that those dying there, far from going to heaven, were reborn as donkeys—and he wanted to debunk the belief. According to him, if one went to heaven merely by dying in Banaras, why would one need the intercession of God?

The sun is now directly overhead. I become impatient to get back to familiar surroundings. Rajghat too is Banaras, but somehow it doesn't feel like it. Historians will tell you that the city originated around here, and if that's the case—well, that *is* the case—Banaras has merely followed the mysterious pattern you find in the growth of cities. A city, once it is born, grows southwards, and as times passes, the south becomes upscale and north down-market. Then one fine day someone recognises the heritage value of the north and people begin flocking to it as part of conducted tours. That time hasn't yet come for Rajghat.

23.

IN SEPTEMBER 1940, when the Second World War was raging, a British ship sailed in convoy from Liverpool, headed for Montreal. Its passengers included 90 evacuated children who were being sent to Canada so that they could escape the German air attacks on Britain. Five days into its journey, it was torpedoed by the German submarine *U-48*. Of the 407 on board, 260 died. The dead included 77 of the 90 children. The ship was called *City of Benares*.

And now, at four this afternoon, the sun still bright but benign, I am sitting at Darbhanga Ghat, watching the city of Banaras come alive. Tourists are emerging from their lodgings. Fake sadhus have taken their positions. There are more boats on the river than I can count.

A Bengali family—three women led by an elderly man—is walking past me. The man is tall and smartly attired: yellow Lacoste T-shirt, black jeans, black cap. They are talking loudly: one of the women is saying that she is feeling much better after her post-lunch nap.

From the opposite direction comes a curly-haired man, and when he overhears the group speaking in Bengali, he exclaims: 'Oh, you people are Bengalis!'

'Yes, indeed,' says the elderly man.

'I am also a Bengali! Where are you from?'

'Calcutta.'

'Great! I am also from Calcutta. Where do you live in Calcutta?'

'Ballygunge.'

'Very good! I live in Garia. How long will you stay in Banaras?'

'Two days. We got in this morning.'

'Which hotel are you staying at?'

The elderly man ignores the question but asks another in return: 'Where in Banaras can I find good Bengali food?'

I don't get to hear the answer because the group has moved away from me, the curly-haired man now walking in the reverse direction along with the fellow Bengalis.

A kite lands on the river. It instantly turns into pulp. But there is a flutter in the water near the spot where the kite crashed. It turns out that a pigeon had got entangled in the kite string. A small crowd gathers around the sight, not quite knowing what to do. A young sadhu—not a fake one—materialises out of nowhere and steps into the river to extricate the bird. He walks away holding the wet pigeon close to his chest.

I get up to have tea. The man running the stall at Darbhanga Ghat makes good tea. Only, he serves it in paper and not clay cups. I had asked him some days ago why he didn't use clay cups, and he had replied something to the effect that he had once been supplied with a consignment of clay cups that were either chipped or cracked, and he had ever since switched to paper cups.

A tall Sikh is already at the stall, waiting for his tea. When he is handed a steaming cup, he regards it with a sneer. 'Such a small cup? Only this much tea?' He is angrier by the second.

'That's all I can give you for five rupees.'

'I don't care about the price. In Punjab, we wouldn't serve tea in such a small cup even to our enemies!'

24.

THE SUN HAS set. Dashashwamedha Ghat is fast filling up with people. Soon, five well-built and photogenic young men will climb up wooden platforms and wave incense and gigantic lamps at the river from a height. For thirty minutes or so, the river will cease to be a river and become Mother Ganga.

For many people, the Ganga Aarti is a spectacle. I find it a sham. I distinctly remember a composite image circulating on Facebook some time ago: it showed a sparkling Thames with the caption, 'When you treat a river like a river', and a dirty Ganga with the caption, 'When you treat a river like a mother'. In Banaras they cleanse their souls—in addition to clothes and buffaloes—in the river all day and in the evening wave lights at it. Those lamps are pyres of irony.

Banaras has today become synonymous with Ganga Aarti. Pilgrims and tourists plan their day around it. Many spend a small fortune to watch it from boats that swarm the Dashashwamedha at the appointed hour. They go back home ecstatic: one more box on their bucket-list ticked off.

The only time I had been a willing spectator was on the day I cremated my mother. The sun had faded by the time my brother and I took dips in the Ganga at Manikarnika after having consigned her navel to the river. Then all of us—my brother, father and my wife—walked from Manikarnika to Dashashwamedha, where the aarti was about to begin. We sat through the ritual; it served as an equivalent of shavasana, the relaxing corpse pose you adopt after a sweaty session of yoga.

This evening there are countless more people at the Dashashwamedha than there had been six years ago. A pre-recorded bhajan begins to play over the loudspeakers as the five young men in yellow robes take up position. Hundreds of phone cameras are switched on. Flashbulbs pop from the boats on the river. The river, for this moment at least, is not melted ice flowing from the Himalayas but gushing straight from the matted locks of Shiva.

Ganga, the story goes, used to be the river of the heavens. The great King Bhagiratha was determined to bring the river to earth to wash away the remains of his 60,000 ancestors who had been reduced to ashes in a flash by the angry gaze of a sage. (Why they were turned into a heap of ashes is another story.) Bhagiratha stood in the Himalaya mountains for a thousand years with his arms raised in prayer to plead with Brahma, the creator, who finally appeared before the king and said that he would have a word with Ganga. But there was a problem: the force of the great river's descent would destroy the earth and Shiva alone was capable of breaking the fall. So Bhagiratha stood for another thousand years, this time on one leg, in order to please Shiva, who was impressed by his determination and agreed to absorb the first gigantic impact of the river. Ganga, as she descended, didn't quite like the idea of being obstructed by Shiva; she decided to push him to the bottom of the earth with her might. But Shiva read her mind and trapped her in the locks of his hair. Bhagiratha, who was watching all this, pleaded with him to release her. After some persuasion, Shiva freed Ganga and let her fall on earth. She followed Bhagiratha's chariot to the spot where the ashes of his great ancestors lay. As soon as the water washed away the ashes, the 60,000 souls were liberated. Their entry into heaven was personally confirmed to Bhagiratha by Brahma, who also announced that, henceforth, the Ganga would water not just heaven but also the earth.

What Dashashwamedha is witnessing now is the marriage of geology and mythology. We are all guests at the wedding.

25.

DASHASHWAMEDHA GHAT EMPTIES out rapidly once the show comes to an end. Locals are now sauntering in. On their faces I detect the relief that comes when you have just seen off a large number of guests from your home—or maybe I am imagining it.

Many Banarasis I have spoken to resent the crowds that pour in for the Ganga Aarti; they don't like the idea of tourists overrunning their city. But the owners of shops that line the road leading from Dashashwamedha all the way to Godowlia are happy.

I stop at the first shop from the ghat to buy a tiny brass lingam—a to-be souvenir from Banaras. And this being Banaras, I soon find myself engaged in conversation with the shopkeeper. His name is Sumit Mishra.

'As far as I remember,' he tells me, 'the aarti began in 1996. For a few years before that, a well-known pandit called Satyendra Mishra had been performing an aarti on a small scale at (the adjacent) Shitala Ghat. In 1996, he shifted the aarti to Dashashwamedha and began holding it in a grand manner. It turned out to be a blessing for us. Once upon a time, Dashashwamedha would be deserted by four in the afternoon. But now it sees a second dawn at that time.'

'At four in the afternoon?' a voice interrupts him His elder brother Surendra Kumar has just arrived at the shop. 'This place would be cleared of people only at around eight in the evening and not at four,' the older man clarifies testily, 'and the aarti was started not in 1996 but in 1989, under the aegis of an NGO called Ganga Seva Nidhi, which was founded by Satyendra Mishra.'

Whatever the exact year, the aarti has certainly improved their business—they both agree on that. 'Now look at my shop,' says Surendra, 'it does not have a shutter. The shutter got damaged two years ago in the floods. I don't bother to replace it because the shop is open all the time, except for two hours from midnight, when I cover it with a curtain.'

Tea arrives. Our conversation meanders from politics to religion to the decline in social values. As I prepare to leave, I ask Surendra the price of a rudraksha necklace.

'That will cost you a thousand rupees. The beads are from Nepal—genuine, very good for health.'

'I don't think I have that much cash on me now. I will pick it up tomorrow morning.'

But he has already plucked a piece from the array and placed it around my neck. 'If you can't pay me today does not mean you can't wear it today. Even if you don't pay me, it is fine. Consider it a blessing from Baba Vishwanath.'

I call Surabhi to ask whether she is free to have dinner with me at Pizzeria. She says she isn't free, she is giving lessons to a child in her neighbourhood, but she will meet me tomorrow morning. Even as my mind is still wondering what I should do next—I have the whole evening ahead of me—I find my feet dragging me to the place I want to avoid but feel drawn to.

26.

A CALF IS licking the belly of a dog. The dog feels ticklish and moves away. The calf follows it. They go around in circles. The dog gives in and they snuggle together, unmindful of the heat generated by the burning pyres nearby, and undisturbed by the funeral processions coming down the steps. They are telling the mourners that life must go on.

I have never seen anyone wail or shed silent tears at Manikarnika. Mourners draw courage and comfort from the sight of several pyres burning simultaneously. As they stand in the heat and smoke, realisation dawns on them that death is a part of life. Something that residents of Manikarnika know from the time they are born. For many of them, death is their livelihood.

'Do you get a stench?' Ajay Dubey, the wood-seller, asks me.

'I do smell something. I recognise Manikarnika by this smell.'

'Yes, but do you get the stench of burning bodies?'

'I am not sure. Maybe I don't.'

'You won't. Bodies burning in Banaras don't give off a smell. That's the beauty of Banaras.'

'Really?'

'Even the smoke from the pyres does you no harm. My father inhaled the smoke all his life, he is over eighty now and he is fine. I have inhaled it all my life, I am also fine.'

Dubey is seated on a cot next to a weighing scale, surrounded by neatly stacked logs of wood. He watches bodies burning all day. He has to. He is in competition with about a dozen other shops at Manikarnika that also sell wood for building pyres.

The wood is usually sold in fixed quantities: five mann, seven mann, nine mann and eleven. Mourners have to make a choice depending on the size of the deceased. One mann equals 40 kg, and the pyre of a well-built adult usually requires nine mann, or 360 kg, of wood. If you use nine mann, says Dubey, '*body achchhe se jalta hai*'—the body burns properly. Each mann costs about 400 rupees.

'Where does the wood come from?' I ask him.

'From the jungles of Madhya Pradesh. The sandalwood comes from Mysore.'

'You sell sandalwood too?'

'Pure sandalwood, 3,000 rupees a kilo. Not everybody can afford it, of course. Only prime ministers and maharajas and the like.'

I do the math: if one mann of wood comes for 400 rupees, nine mann would cost 3,600 rupees. Add to that the fee of the priest and the doam who tends the pyre. So a cremation should cost around 5,000 rupees? Even though I had lit my mother's pyre right here six years ago, I had no idea about the expenses because they had been taken care of by my brother's colleagues, who were repaid later.

'No, it would cost more,' says Dubey. 'You also have to buy the fire. There's an eternal flame burning up there,' he points to an ancient temple next to us.

I've noticed the temple before. The Shiva there—known as Mahakaal, the timeless—overlooks the pyres and the river. But I had no idea an eternal fire burns there.

'How much does the fire cost?'

'It's not fixed. The doam raja usually gauges the financial condition of the mourner before quoting a price.'

He asks one of the boys at his shop to guide me to the fire.

Before I leave, I gather that Dubey runs another shop upstairs. That shop sells musical instruments: tabla, sitar, flute. *Dekh tamasha lakdi ka*. Standing here, though, you almost forget that wood is capable of things other than burning a body. Such as producing music.

The boy taking me to see the eternal fire is called Kailash. He leads me up a short flight of stairs into a soot-coated sandstone structure that is not exactly a part of the temple but which seems all the same to be supporting it. Here, on a stone bench in a corner, a small pile of wood is smouldering angry red—the eternal fire. In another corner is a cot and seated on it a chubby man in a yellow shirt and brown trousers. He has a ringside view of the burning ghat but right now he is looking at his phone. On his lap rests a plastic pouch packed with paan. He is the doam raja. Well, he isn't the raja himself but a member of the raja's family and at the moment the boss of Manikarnika. He is the one authorised to provide fire for cremations. His name is Onkar Chaudhari.

Onkar is twenty-nine years old. He appears to be the shy sort. I ask him if his job has altered his outlook on life.

He ponders over my question for a few moments and replies: 'All I can say is that I don't want my children to be doing this job. I have made sure they go to school.'

'I didn't mean that,' I tell him, 'what I mean is, since you deal with the dead all the time, do you look at life any differently?'

'I just told you. I don't want my children to be sitting here when they grow up.'

'I'm told that there is only one truth in life,' I try to make myself clearer, 'anyone who is born has to die. You encounter that truth every moment. Does that make you regard life any differently from others?'

'I am not here all the time. We take turns. When I am not assigned to this place, I don't think of death. I go back to the world of *moh maya* (attachment). And let me tell you one thing. While it is true that anyone who is born has to die, there is no guarantee that everyone who dies gets a cremation. There are people who die but their bodies are never found. When such families come to us, we make a human figure out of flour and cremate it so that their soul rests in peace.'

We are soon joined by Onkar's elder brother Jairaja Chaudhari. We exchange pleasantries. Unlike his brother, Jairaja is dressed conservatively and carries himself like a Hindi-belt politician: white kurta and pajama, with a gamchha around his neck. They have two other brothers, who will replace these two in the mornings. The family of the doam raja is a large one: the four brothers will be on duty at Manikarnika for ten days, after which another set of cousins will take over, and it will be four months before the turn of these brothers comes round again.

Since the raja's family is concentrated in Manikarnika and Harishchandra Ghat, the dead remain a part of their life even when they are not on cremation duty. 'We are used to dead bodies,' says Onkar, laconically. 'When I sit here late in the night, and there is total silence, I can still hear "*Ram naam satya hai*" even if there is no procession coming in. That may be because my ears want to hear it, because the chant is our source of income.'

'How much do you charge for the fire?'

'There is no fixed price,' says Jairaja. 'It depends on what the mourner is capable of spending. It can be as low as 51 rupees and it can be as high as—'

'As high as?'

'As I said, it's not fixed. It can be 51 rupees, 501 rupees, 1,001 rupees, 2,001 rupees and so on.'

'Is it true that the navel doesn't burn during cremation?'

'That's not true,' says Onkar. 'Everything burns. We deliberately save some part of the body to be consigned to the river. The human body is made up of five elements which include water, therefore some part of your body must go back to water or else you don't get salvation. Are you a Bengali?'

'That's right.'

'Bengalis save the navel. Other people save other parts. Usually a few pieces of bone are saved for the river—the ribs of men and the hip bones of women.'

'Has there been any incident at the ghat that especially remains in your memory?' I ask him.

Onkar looks at Jairaja: 'Tell him about the chachi episode.'

Jairaja says, 'Many years ago, they brought this woman for cremation. Her nephew was in the procession and he was inconsolable. He was drunk too. He loved his chachi (aunt) so much that he couldn't bear the sight of her body being set on fire. He jumped into the pyre. And died in it.

'There is another incident, which took place one winter at Harishchandra Ghat. An elderly woman was brought in for cremation, and when the body was taken to the river for washing before it could be placed on the pyre, the old lady began shivering. She was rushed to the hospital, where doctors found her heart to be beating. Her family gave her a sweet, which she ate, and within a matter of minutes, she was dead.'

We exchange numbers as I get up to leave. Jairaja tells me, 'Since you are writing about us, don't forget to mention that people belonging to our caste do not get rid of female foetuses and do not give or ask for dowry.'

Bells from nearby temples are tolling. Another funeral procession is coming down the steps: '*Ram naam satya hai*!' The wood crackles as the flames leap out of the pyres. The cocktail of these sounds—offset by the calm of the river—must have represented Manikarnika from the time it came into existence—how long ago, only Mahakaal will know. All one can determine is that Manikarnika continues to be driven by the oldest discovery in the history of mankind: fire.

I stand by the pyres along with Kailash, the boy who had led me to the eternal fire. A bull is sitting next to us, sagaciously watching the proceedings.

'How old are you, Kailash?'

'I am twenty-eight.'

'Really? I thought you'd be seventeen or eighteen.'

'I look that young?' he grins. 'I guess it's the grace of Lord Shiva.'

Kailash's father too works in the wood shop, but of late he has developed a heart ailment and is mostly confined to home, looked after by Kailash's mother. Kailash has four brothers: the two elder to him are boatmen, and the younger two employed in grocery shops. The family lives at Manikarnika. Most of Kailash's time is spent in the service of Dubey, the wood-seller. In the mornings he helps out at the shop that sells musical instruments, in the evenings he comes down to load wood onto the weighing scale. Occasionally, he gets to show tourists around. Since he has no education—he has not even been to school—he cannot find a better job.

'I have no complaints,' says Kailash, 'I am a typical Banarasi. I believe in being happy.'

'Don't you find it depressing to watch bodies burning all the time?'

'Far from it,' he laughs. 'Death is inevitable. We all have to go one day. So why not be happy as long as we are alive? Why burden yourself with tension. And let me tell you, for me the pyres are a way of life. I have known no other life. I even pluck wood from burning pyres during the winter and take it home to keep warm.'

'Really?' I am unable to hide my surprise.

'Not only that, sometimes I carry burning wood home even to cook. Only last night we cooked rice and daal and chokha on wood from a pyre. I have no shame in telling you that.'

'Shame? I would say you are Shiva!'

27.

'GOD CREATED KASHI,' says the boatman, 'then the Ganga came and the sun decided to shine on the city. That's how it all began.'

It must have begun that way. Without God, Ganga and the sun, there would be no Kashi, no City of Light.

At the moment, there is no sun, but it is going to show up any moment. Surabhi and I have taken a boat from Assi and are headed for the opposite bank. There's nothing out there, but we are still going there because—well, there is no reason at all.

For that matter, there's hardly anything to see in Banaras. It has neither the charm of the hills nor the calm of the sea; it has a river in which people wash away their sins, its galis are narrow enough to induce claustrophobia, and on two of its ghats human flesh is constantly turning into ash. Banaras, that way, is ugliness personified. Yet people return, from time to time, from far and near. What is it about Banaras?

I remember a joke my father told me many, many years ago. A man is searching for something under a street lamp. A passerby asks him what he is looking for. 'I have lost my watch,' the man replies. 'Where did you lose it?' the passerby asks. 'Out there,' the man points to a dark stretch. 'Then why are you looking for it here?' the surprised passerby asks. 'That's because there is light here,' the man replies.

That's what it is about Banaras. People who think they're lost come here to find themselves because there is light here.

The sky, grey a few moments ago, is slowly turning pink. Surabhi and I step onto the white sands. She has been exceptionally silent today. I ask her now if something is the matter.

'Nothing,' she shakes her head. 'When are you coming back to Banaras?'

'I wish I knew. Let's take pictures of ourselves here.'

We click numerous pictures, the river and the ghats spread out behind us. Now I discover the purpose of having come here: to watch the river and the city in one frame at sunrise. Just like an oil lamp highlights the facial features of a stone idol on the altar, the sun is now lighting up the sandstone structures that constitute the face of Banaras.

The thing with Banaras, and not with any other city, is that it has looked nearly the same over the decades, if not centuries. Whether it's the photograph-like pencil sketches of James Prinsep, who carried out the first-ever survey of the city in the 1820s ('This is a glorious sight, to see the ghats of Benares covered with a moving sea of heads, studded at small distances with temples of white and red stone'); whether it's scenes from Satyajit Ray's *Joi Baba Felunath*; or the pictures you see on Instagram—the Banaras in them hardly varies.

There will come a time, perhaps, when this appearance would have lived out its lifespan and the riverfront would begin to look different. But that's unlikely to happen before many more generations have attained salvation at Manikarnika.

Back at Assi I say goodbye to Surabhi. She has to rush to college. I too need to get back to pack my bags. Since I am not in a great hurry, I climb up the steps at Tulsi Ghat to take a look at Tulsidas's akhara—it's called the Swaminath Akhara—just in case I find men wrestling there.

Sure enough, the place is packed with langoti-clad men. One of them is doing pushups, palms placed on bricks. Another is doing dumbbell curls. Yet another is hoisting himself up and down on the parallel bars.

On the wrestling pit, overlooked by a shrine of Lord Hanuman, are two pairs of young men, each pair locked in a contest. Passing tips to them is a much older man who is seated under a tree, wearing a T-shirt and langoti. Since the T-shirt is long, it looks as if he is naked waist below. Introducing myself, I sit next to him and ask him if the mud in the wrestling pit is indeed beneficial for health.

'This is no ordinary mud,' he tells me. 'It is mixed with mustard oil, turmeric, alum, curd, and neem leaves. It keeps all sorts of skin diseases at bay, and if you roll in it, your body is energised. Boys who work out in modern gyms are no match for our boys.'

The man's name is Siyaram. I am surprised when I learn his age—sixty-two—because he looks trim and strong and not older than forty-five. He lives in Durgakund, his family has been in Banaras for several generations.

He tells me: 'I have been coming here from the age of fourteen. I used to wrestle earlier. Wrestling was my hobby. I would watch others and learn. Some of the legendary wrestlers, such as Mewa Pehelwan and Kallu Pehelwan, were produced by this akhara. I have seen them practise here.

'I don't wrestle anymore, but I still come here every single day to work out with the boys and to give them guidance. I do pushups, I do sit-ups, I do some weights. Exercise gives you the confidence to face life.

'My life has been very hard. I lost my father when I was in the first standard. I had practically no clothes to wear, hardly any food to eat. My mother worked in other people's homes to bring me up. I could study only up to the tenth standard, but for poor people like us, that was not a small thing in those days.

'After I left school, I joined the LIC (Life Insurance Corporation of India) as a daily-wager. Soon they made me a chaprasi (peon), then after many years I became a clerk, and finally retired as an assistant. Life wasn't easy in spite of the job. My wife had to stitch clothes to earn some extra money because we had three children to look after.

'But, despite the hardships, I never asked anyone for help or money. I still never do. You must have the courage to face difficulties. You must have the courage to face disease. A lot of that courage came because of my regular practice at the akhara. I never missed a day. When you follow a routine, and stick to it come what may, everything falls into place.'

'What is your routine like?'

'You should follow a routine that gives you satisfaction. Otherwise it becomes forced and difficult to stick to. In my case I get up at four every morning and the first thing I do is sweep my room and the courtyard with a broom and then dust the furniture and windows with a gamchha. Using a broom is beneficial for your health: it keeps your hips flexible. Once I am done with the cleaning, I share a glass of tea with my wife. That's another ritual I have followed without fail.

'Then I come to the akhara, spend a couple of hours here, return home to bathe and after that visit the temples at Durgakund and also the Sankat Mochan Temple. I return home for breakfast and eat whatever is served to me imagining it to be the best breakfast in the world. That's how my attitude has been all along. I eat whatever is served to me—even if it is just salt and roti—thinking it is the *best* food in the world.

'After breakfast I go to my shop. It is a grocery shop, run by my two sons, the oldest and the youngest. I have three sons. The one in the middle is a lawyer. Our financial troubles are behind us now, I am a happy man. But I was happy even during the difficult days because I was always satisfied with whatever little I had. I never asked anyone for favours. Satisfaction is the most important thing in life. If you have satisfaction, you have everything.'

That's my takeaway message from this trip to Banaras: satisfaction is everything. All these days I was rubbing shoulders with sadhus on the ghats, but finally, on the day of my departure, I have come across a sage, that too in a gym.

PART TWO

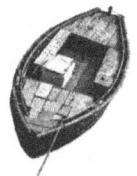

28.

I AM BACK after three years.

Three years is a fraction of a second in the life of Banaras. It is not a very long time in the life of a human either, but considering that every moment is potentially life-changing, many things can happen in three years to make the period look long.

Surabhi is now married and has left Banaras. Akanksha too is married and she has also left Banaras. *Mohalla Assi*, the movie based on *Kashi ka Assi*, has finally made it to the theatres: it was released just a couple of weeks ago. My own life has undergone a change, drastic enough to be recorded in another book but best forgotten. There have been smaller changes too: back then, Chennai was my home, now I live in Calcutta; back then I couldn't do without my evening drinks, now I am a teetotaller.

My previous visit to Banaras seems distant; my earlier visits feel remote and even unreal. When I had flown down to cremate my mother back in 2009, the road leading from the airport to the city belonged to the countryside. Now, in the winter of 2018, when I've arrived in an evening flight from Calcutta, I find the same road lined with specialty hospitals (the new business in India), hotels and shopping malls (one of them has stocked brands such as Armani and G-Star). The airport itself has undergone transformation beyond belief.

But neither the airport nor the road leading to the city belongs to what's quintessentially Banaras, where the rickety wooden boat is often the fastest mode of transport. Once the cab drops me off near Godowlia, I see very little has changed. After checking into the hotel—built just two years ago, the only noticeable addition to the Godowlia intersection—I walk down to Dashashwamedha to find Banaras just the way I had left it.

The boatmen I had encountered when they were boys must be young adults now, but I find other boys pestering me for a ride. A fake sadhu, every inch of his skin covered in ash, shields his face with a newspaper when I aim my phone-camera at him: he doesn't want to be photographed for free. Was he there during my last visit? I suspect he was. Boys are playing cricket as usual, though this time I also see girls playing badminton on a makeshift court. Pilgrims are posing for pictures. The signboard of Banaras Sari Factory remains untouched by the sun or the rain. A cow is looking for something to munch on. A dog has pounced upon another dog for intruding into its territory.

It feels as if I had got up from my desk mid-sentence to answer the doorbell and have returned now to resume writing.

29.

BUT NO, ONE major change *is* taking place in Banaras.

Around the Vishwanath Temple—the temple of the Destroyer—systematic destruction is taking place on a scale the city hasn't witnessed since the time of Aurangzeb.

In the name of beautification, a strip of land between the temple and the Manikarnika is being cleared of all buildings, many as old as the temple itself, for the construction of a corridor that will benefit tourists and pilgrims. Soon they won't have to jostle through the narrow alleys to reach the temple but can stroll from the river to the temple, and vice versa, on a 'beautiful' corridor that will have restrooms and greenery and be wide enough to see ambulances and fire tenders through in case of emergencies.

Close to 300 structures are being flattened for this project, a brainchild of Prime Minister Modi and being implemented with an iron hand by the government of Uttar Pradesh, where his party, the rightwing Bharatiya Janata Party or BJP, is in power. Needless to say, some of the oldest mohallas—neighbourhoods—of Banaras are wiped out.

The destruction isn't immediately apparent if you have just arrived in Banaras. It is visible from gate no. 4 of the temple, which I stroll to the following morning.

The alley adjoining this side of the temple resembles a freshly-bombed street in Syria, bathed in sunlight because the buildings that stood on it are now rubble.

The demolition has also brought into view the domes of the Vishwanath Temple and the Aurangzeb-built Gyanvapi mosque. So far they weren't visible from a distance, but one has a clear idea now where the original temple stood and where the new one was later built.

I walk deeper into the alley—into more destruction. Labourers are hammering away with all their might at stone and mortar. Alleys of Banaras are still too narrow for bulldozers. I stop at a two-storeyed building whose ground floor serves as a sari shop. It is one of the few buildings that still stand on that stretch: the others are already rubble or hollowed out.

Gathered on the steps of the shop are a few men, including Ajay Kapoor, its owner, whose large family lives upstairs. His employees are packing up the saris before the labourers arrive with their hammers. With his family business winding up and his family home about to be razed, Kapoor, now in his fifties, will have to start from scratch in another corner of Banaras.

Since he is pitted against the might of the administration, there is nothing he can do about it, and therefore he has very little to do now other than while away his time with his equally disconsolate neighbours. This luxury—of idling with neighbours, a typically Banarasi pastime—will not be available to him once he finally moves out. When I join the men, tea materialises.

This neighbourhood is—rather *was*—called Lahori Tola. The first folk to settle here had migrated from Lahore during the time of Maharaja Ranjit Singh, who had donated the gold that adorns the temple's dome.

Aimless in Banaras

Today, their descendants find the ground being pulled from under their feet.

'We no longer call it Lahori Tola, we call it Swargiya (Late) Lahori Tola. It has been wiped out by an earthquake—the Modi earthquake,' says Ajay Kapoor with a bitter laugh. He has always voted for the BJP, but now he is angry with the PM: 'He doesn't care about these losses because 300 houses add up to only a few thousand votes; he can do without those votes.'

His neighbours begin to speak:

'Modi considers Banaras to be his personal property. Does he realise that Banaras is not just a city, but a culture? Galis are part of that culture. Soon you won't find us here, sitting and chatting. This gali will be gone, there will be a corridor.'

'They say they are building the corridor to prevent stampedes. Tell me, have you ever heard of a stampede in Banaras?'

'Modi wants to turn Banaras into Kyoto, to bring in more tourists. Why should they come to Banaras then, they would rather go to Kyoto.'

'They forced us to sell our properties. No consultation, no warning, no hearing, they just came and said, "Surrender your property to Bholenath."'

'The media is to be blamed equally. They never highlighted our plight.'

These men have received compensation from the government—they don't reveal how much—but they say the amount got divided among so many family members that each got only a pittance.

Kapoor offers a hypothetical example, although it sounds more like his own case: 'Let us say, a house gets one crore rupees as compensation. Sounds huge, right?

But there are five brothers living in that house, so each brother gets only 20 lakh rupees. With your business shut and no roof over your head, can you start life all over again with just 20 lakh?'

Presently a sunburned man walks in and, with a sigh, seats himself amidst us. His name is Sanjay Singh, as I can tell from his identity card, and he is one of the contractors entrusted with the demolition. More tea is sent for.

Sanjay Singh too is an unhappy man: in the past three months he has demolished four buildings, two of which he has rendered 'fresh', but the government is yet to pay him for his services. By 'fresh' he means complete clearance: demolition as well as removal of debris. 'I was hoping to be paid before Diwali, but Diwali has come and gone and there is still no sign of payment,' he laments, sipping dourly on the tea.

Both Sanjay Singh and I are people the residents of erstwhile Lahori Tola could be forgiven for shooing away, yet they shifted aside to make space for us to sit and also gave us tea. That's Banaras.

I resume my journey through the alley, making my way past dust and past various stages of destruction. In many places I see a temple standing amid the debris. The emergence of these temples—most of them contemporaries of the Vishwanath Temple—from many of the demolished structures has given a moral edge to the government, which now says that the razed structures were encroachments and shouldn't have existed in the first place.

It is a different matter that the government had no idea about the presence of these temples when it ordered the demolition; and it is not clear what it intends to do with them, now that it has been established—by the Archaeological Survey of India—that they have heritage value. For that matter, even the razed structures, whether encroachments or not, had acquired heritage value because they sheltered several generations of Banarasis.

I emerge at the Lalita Ghat, to the smell of burning pyres drifting from the neighbouring Manikarnika. I climb up to the Nepali Temple, where I sight ghosts of younger versions of Surabhi and me. On the river I spot something new. Migratory birds, hundreds of them, are sitting in formations on the water—white patterns on green. Winter is a good time to be in Banaras.

I walk to Dashashwamedha, where I have sandwiches at Shree Café and make friends with its owner, Santosh Pandey. The café functions out of his home, 150 years old, built by his great-grandfather who had migrated from Rajasthan, where he was the royal astrologer.

Pandey, as a boy, flew kites, played chess, played the sarod, grew up to try his hand at many businesses without much luck, and then, about twenty years ago, opened this café which—'with the blessings of Lord Vishwanath'—has turned out to be a success.

Nearly all the diners, I notice, are Westerners. Pandey's menu boasts of several continental dishes apart from the regular Indian curries. The food, he says, tastes like what they eat at home because the clients are constantly sharing recipes with the cook, even taking the liberty of walking into the kitchen to demonstrate cooking techniques.

'We are like one big family,' says Pandey, 'all kinds of people come to eat here—chefs, artists, photographers, writers, journalists—most of them are artists at heart.'

The café keeps him busy nearly all day but he still finds time to pursue his current passion, photography. Of late he has been chronicling the disappearance of the section of Banaras I've just walked through. Buildings that are no longer there, or soon won't be there, are preserved in his camera.

He tells me, 'The other day, when I was out taking pictures, a shopkeeper, whose shop is gone, told me, "Modi has achieved what Alauddin Khilji and Aurangzeb couldn't. He has demolished homes of Hindus." My house is safe as of now, but who knows what they will come up with next?'

'Didn't people protest?'

'They did, but they didn't find enough support.'

It's not difficult to guess why: those untouched by the project have remained indifferent to the plight of those displaced. During the course of the morning I came across several Banarasis who, to my surprise, hailed the demolition. They said most of the buildings razed were not occupied by their owners but by tenants who had been paying a measly rent for decades, and that the owners were only too happy to get rid of their properties along with occupants.

Pandey lives close enough to the proposed corridor to be concerned. Even a minor alteration in the plan can displace him as well. 'Every night,' he says, 'I hear the clopping of the donkeys carrying away the debris. It's a very distressing sound, believe me.'

He then pulls out his phone to show me a video clip of a gathering in which a theatre artiste can be heard lamenting, 'What you see being carried away by the donkeys is not debris but Banaras.'

Aimless in Banaras

Later in the afternoon, in his office located in the Vishwanath Temple complex, I meet Vishal Singh, the young bureaucrat who, as the CEO of the temple, is executing the corridor project. Many in Banaras hate him today, many others admire him. His dress sense is certainly admirable.

The clean-shaven officer cuts an impressive figure in a white shirt and grey suit. One wall in his office has a blown-up satellite image of riverside Banaras and several CCTV screens capturing every single movement inside the temple. By his desk sits a large brass Nandi, the bull, wearing a rose garland.

'Change is always turbulent,' he tells me, 'but if you say change cannot happen, I will not buy that.'

'Exactly whose brainchild is the project?' I ask him.

'It would be very difficult for me to pinpoint. All I can tell you is that the plan was conceived in 2007. I would even say that the idea dates back to 1916 when Mahatma Gandhi visited the temple and was appalled by the filth and congestion around it. [Modi] has only provided a fillip to the project.'

Singh does not think the people who have been displaced are unhappy: 'I have paid them twice the circle rate. For them, it's like this: "If I am compensated well enough, why not move on. I am not giving up anything, I am merely transacting business." You should talk to people who are not biased.'

He also dismisses the idea that the demolition has altered the character of Banaras. 'Of the 1,700 galis in Banaras I have touched only these two,' he runs his finger along the map placed on his desk.

Both the galis in question emerge from the temple complex: one leads to Lalita Ghat and the other to Manikarnika. They are being merged into the corridor and everything standing in-between is going—or already gone.

'Please understand that we need such a corridor. At present, if there is a fire or stampede, only God can help us,' he says.

'Now that I am here,' I tell him, 'can I have a quick darshan of Lord Vishwanath?'

'Why quick? Make it a long one, if you like.'

Singh hands me over to an aide, who escorts me out of the office and in turn hands me over to a police constable.

The constable first takes me to the sanctum sanctorum, where a priest picks up a marigold garland resting on the lingam and flings it at me. Then he shows me the now-levelled Gyanvapi well. The priest of the original temple is said to have thrown the lingam into this well to save it from Aurangzeb's men; some say the priest had jumped into the well along with the lingam. From here Aurangzeb's mosque is clearly visible, an imposing three-domed structure, separated from the present temple complex by tall iron railings.

'Look what the Muslims did,' the constable points to the base of the mosque, where the remains of the old temple can still be seen. 'What happened was bad, very bad.'

History becomes clearer now: the Vishwanath Temple stood there until 1669, when Aurangzeb demolished it to build the mosque, and in 1780 Ahilyabai Holkar rebuilt the temple on the spot we are standing now.

The 'original' temple wasn't the original one either. Vishwanath Temple had been demolished—and rebuilt—a couple of times before. Banaras, clearly, is not a stranger to destruction. Invaders have come and gone, regimes installed and toppled, edifices built and razed, but Banaras has gone on. It will go on.

30.

'NOW, THIS IS Banaras,' Abhay Tripathi gestures to me. Abhay and I are standing on a terrace overlooking the Panchganga Ghat and he is pointing to a sight that has many things in one frame. There is the Ganga, green and serene, the boats on it encircled by migratory birds looking to be fed. There is the temple of Trailanga Swami, the walking Shiva of Kashi. And towering behind the temple is a seventeenth-century mosque, from where a stream of boys emerges wearing skullcaps. The boys, being boys, are now sprinting down the steps of the mosque, built by Aurangzeb over a Vishnu temple.

'I am a devout Hindu,' says Abhay, 'I even went to Ayodhya in December 1992 to pull down the Babri mosque. But I am not against Muslims. They are as much a part of Banaras as we are.'

Abhay is exactly my age and, like me, a journalist, but, unlike me, knows the alleys of Banaras like the back of his hand.

'In 2006,' he says, 'when there was a blast at the Sankat Mochan temple, more Muslims than Hindus had volunteered to donate blood to the injured. The blast took place in the evening, but everything was cleaned up in a matter of hours and worship resumed, as usual, at the crack of dawn next morning. That's the beauty of this city.'

'You say you are not against Muslims—what made you go to Ayodhya, then?'

'I strongly believe that a Ram temple should be built there. Moreover, the Babri mosque was not even in use, Muslims weren't offering prayers there.'

'Didn't your family oppose the idea of you going there?'

'They did, but I wanted to go because I was young, and the public mood was in favour of the temple. On the night of December 5 (1992), some fifteen of us went to the station to take the train to Ayodhya. At the station, five or six people in the group went back home under pressure from their families. The rest of us got onto a train coming from Sealdah and bound for Delhi. We reached Ayodhya in the morning, freshened up and headed for the Babri mosque. The BJP leaders—L.K. Advani, Murli Manohar Joshi and others—were making their speeches. Around 12.30 p.m., kar sewaks climbed up the three domes of the mosque and began to demolish them.'

'Were you among those who climbed the domes?'

'No, I was among those standing below, cheering the ones on top.

'Once the first dome crashed, at about 1.30, I decided to leave because I had done my bit. There was thick dust in the air. I ran into the chief photographer of *Aaj* newspaper. At the time my father worked in that paper, in the administrative department, and I was to join it later as a journalist. The photographer's camera had got smashed in the commotion but he pulled out the roll and handed it over to me. He asked me to take it safely to the *Aaj* offices in Banaras. I walked back to the railway station. Actually, I didn't have to walk; I got pushed by the crowd all the way to the station. I reached Banaras around

10.30 in the night, well in time before the newspaper was put to bed.'

'After all these years, do you regret going to Ayodhya?'

'No, I don't. I told you, I am a devout Hindu. But I don't like what the BJP government is currently doing in Banaras. Many mohallas have vanished because of the corridor project. Families that lived together for generations have been separated. Five brothers living together in one building will now have to find five different houses because it is simply impossible for them to find a modern construction large enough to accommodate the families of all five. If Modi wanted development, he should have looked at places around Banaras that are not developed. He shouldn't have tampered with tradition.'

'Tell me, why did people vote for Modi, who is not even a Banarasi but from Gujarat?'

'That's the beauty of Banaras. No one is really an outsider. We have a mini-Gujarat in Banaras, just as we have a mini-Bengal and a mini-Rajasthan. But no one should take Banaras for granted. *Yeh sheher chadata bhi hai, utaarta bhi hai.*'—The city can put you on a pedestal, but it can also bring you down.

Then, surveying the expanse of the river, he adds: '*Yeh ajeeb sheher hai, bada mast sheher hai*'—Banaras is a strange city, but one that is happy-go-lucky.

31.

ONE THING I like about my hotel—called Ganges Grand—is that its dining hall offers a ringside view of the Godowlia intersection minus the noise.

The intersection, marked by a column supporting Shiva's bull, is the heart of Banaras. Each day at least 25,000 pilgrims pour into the city, and they must get to Godowlia first in order to find their way to the various ghats and temples. So every morning, over breakfast, I watch from the sealed window the heart pumping blood into the arteries of Banaras. The sight also prepares me for the plunge, because minutes later I will be a part of the same bustle I had been witnessing from the window.

How does it feel to be in the bustle? An accurate analogy would be difficult to offer, but it feels somewhat like being in the midst of a busy railway station: trains are constantly arriving and departing, people are boarding and alighting. A more appropriate comparison has just occurred to me. If the train to moksha departs from Banaras, then Godowlia is the lone ticket window where a few thousand hands are shoved in at all times—you can imagine the noise.

At nights when I retire to my windowless room—there is a window, but it's meant to stay shut—the noise stays in my ears for a long, long time. And when the ears adjust to the silence, I wonder if that's the sound of salvation.

But right now it is broad daylight and I've just stepped out of the hotel. I am greeted by a man whom I am unable to place immediately, but as he begins to make polite enquiries, I recall him to be the taxi driver who had brought me from the airport to the hotel. Throughout the journey he had been asking me questions like a curious child, and even now he has something he wants to know.

'Why do we see so many policewomen these days, sir?'

A group of young policewomen is walking past us.

'That's because policemen are not supposed to deal with women,' I tell him.

'You are right. If a policeman deals with a woman, she can always accuse him of rape. This has become very common these days—women accusing men of rape even when rape doesn't happen.'

'Sometimes rape does happen.'

'Tell me, sir, why do men rape?'

'That's a difficult question. Tell me, what are you doing here at the hotel?'

'I am supposed to drop a guest to the airport. Tell me, sir, are women raped when they wear skimpy clothes?'

'You think so?'

'I think so. If they wear saris, they may not be raped. Do you want to buy saris?'

'No, I have no intention of buying saris.'

'Some of the well-known sari shops are gone, unfortunately. They have been demolished because of the corridor project.'

'Such a terrible thing, isn't it?'

'Why terrible? It is a good thing. Those buildings were all encroachments.'

'But several mohallas that stood for more than 100 years are gone.'

'So what, sir? *Tootega tabhi toh banega*'—Only if you destroy can you create.

A man asking me silly questions has suddenly come up with something so profound. *Only if you destroy can you create.* I recently came across exactly the same thought shared on Instagram as a motivational quote, even though I am unable to recall which celebrity it was attributed to.

32.

ONE EVENING, LOOKING to eat something simple instead of the rich curries listed on the hotel menu, I chance upon a man frying freshly-rolled parathas. I find him right in the madness of Godowlia, stationed at the mouth of an arched corridor that seems to be a part of an old house.

I ask him if I can get a cauliflower paratha. 'By all means,' he says, 'please take a seat.' He points to a few plastic chairs placed in the corridor.

Within minutes he hands me a plate containing a hot paratha, a bowl of potato curry of the sort made at home, and coriander chutney.

'Why don't you try some rajma and rice as well?' The voice making the suggestion belongs to a respectable-looking man seated cross-legged on a cement bench built against the wall of the corridor.

'I will, if I am still hungry after eating the paratha.'

'It's homemade. The rajma has come from Uttarakhand, the rice has come from my farm. Try it out.'

'I will.'

The meal turns out to be gratifying, doubly so because the bill is less than fifty rupees.

The respectable-looking man turns out to be the owner of the house. His name is Rajpati Singh. During the day his son uses the corridor to sell Banarasi saris, and in the evening he allows the paratha man to set up his shop.

The paratha man has been in the business for barely two weeks but he is doing well; seeing him do well, Singh decided to add to the variety by including home-cooked food. There's rajma, chana and karhi by rotation—each of them goes well with rice.

Singh tells me: 'This man'—the paratha man—'works in a pharmacy run by my friend and has two daughters who will soon reach marriageable age. He is looking to increase his income so that he can marry them off, so I allowed him to use this space. I don't charge him a paisa.'

'I must say you are very kind.'

'In the Bhagwad Gita, Krishna tells Arjuna: "I am not the first knowledgeable person in this universe and you are not the first seeker. People like you and me have been there before and will come after we are gone." There is nothing new about what I am doing.'

Singh is sixty-five years old. He was born in a village on the outskirts of Banaras and studied political science in BHU. After he completed his master's, he enrolled for a PhD but lost interest in studies within a year. He told his mentor he wanted to quit and be on his own. No employer in the world—he told the guide—ever compensated employees in a fair manner, and he would rather evaluate himself than be evaluated by an employer. But the guide was concerned; he wanted Singh to finish his PhD, take up a teaching job and settle down.

Singh tells me: 'People talk of being settled. How can one settle when you are not even sure of your next breath? I got into the plotting business'—buying farmlands and dividing them into plots for sale—'and became successful. I had promised my guide that I would give him a plot, which I did.

'There is another reason why I didn't want to take up a job. I am the eldest son and had I taken up a job, my father would have sold his farm and moved in with me. I didn't want that to happen. Owning a farm is a matter of prestige; selling it, a loss of prestige. Our farm remained a source of income even as I made money from the plotting business. My wife had a regular job, she taught in a government school.

'I made enough money to buy this house. I bought it some forty years ago from a wealthy Bengali called Raja Jagadish Chandra Sinha, who owned several properties in Banaras. I also fulfilled my responsibility of marrying off the girls in my family. I have an elder sister and four younger sisters and four younger brothers. I have three daughters and a son. I married off all my sisters and my brothers' daughters and also my own daughters. In all, I must have married off thirteen or fourteen girls.

'That is why I could relate to the concern of this man (the paratha-seller) when he told me about his daughters having reached marriageable age, and allowed him to set up shop here. But credit must go to him as well—he works in the pharmacy all day and spends the evenings here selling parathas. Fortunately, his business was good from day one.

'I hope he gets more customers every passing day, which should not be difficult because so many people are coming to Banaras these days. I have never seen so many people before. On the flip side, Godowlia is now congested and polluted. Sometimes I find it difficult to sleep because of the noise. My wife and I are now planning to spend the nights at the village house and return at six in the morning, because enough is enough.'

33.

BACK IN THE hotel, I dip into the books I am carrying with me. Leafing through Kashinath Singh's *Kashi ka Assi* is always like holding to myself the spirit of Banaras. I keep returning to the parts that tickle me. For example, the Banarasi-style definition of a Banarasi: the one who struts about in a carefree fashion, the world placed on his dick. I just saw an example in Mr Singh, who had abandoned his PhD and got into the plotting business because he didn't want to be answerable to a boss.

I now pull out another book from the bedside pile. It's a new book—a recently-published collection of eminent historian Nilakanta Sastri's writings in *The Hindu*—bought only a few days ago at a 10-per-cent discount which I am entitled to as an employee of the paper. To my utter delight, I find an entire piece devoted to the origin of lingam worship.

As expected, the stories vary. One story is that Shiva, emerging from a lake after hiding under water for a long time, finds the universe full of creatures not of his making. In anger he chops off his lingam and throws it into the water. The organ sticks out of the lake in a state of permanent erection.

Another story goes that when Shiva and Dakshayani, newly married, are making love, she finds herself unequal to satisfying him and withdraws. As she withdraws, their reproductive fluids fall to the ground and lingams and yonis sprout all over.

Yet another story, my favourite: Shiva and his wife (Dakshayani reborn as Parvati) are travelling through the air; as they fly over the Daruka forests (Dwarka), Shiva draws her attention to the wives of the sages moving below and praises their devotion to their husbands. Parvati urges her husband to go in the midst of those women as a handsome male and try corrupting their virtue. Shiva obliges, and sure enough, the women fall for him. Shiva resumes his flight, but the sages, when they discover what their wives had been up to, curse that the offending lingam should fall to the ground. Their curse takes effect, leading to a crisis, which is resolved when a compromise is reached: the lingam should be worshipped by all as the highest deity.

While devotees descend on Banaras to worship Shiva's lingam, the quintessential Banarasi has the world placed on his own lingam as he goes about spouting wisdom from his paan-stuffed mouth.

34.

SOMETIMES, ISOLATED OCCURRENCES in life arrange themselves so miraculously into a favourable chain of events that you see it as an act of God. What has just happened to me is nothing short of a miracle.

It was in 2009 that my first book *Chai, Chai*—about life in small towns that serve as big railway junctions—was published. Then, in 2016, its Hindi translation came out. One of its readers happened to be a man called Ramdeo Singh, the chief ticket-examiner at Mughal Sarai station, one of the junctions covered in the book. He wrote to me praising the book and soon afterwards sent me a copy of his newly-published work in Hindi, *Ticket Please*, based on his long experience as a ticket-checker.

What a tragedy, I remember telling myself back then. Had I met Ramdeo Singh in Mughal Sarai when I was writing *Chai, Chai*, the book would have been richer. It would have contained many of the stories that make *Ticket Please* an engaging read. By the time our paths crossed, Ramdeo Singh was on the verge of retirement and was preparing to settle in his village in Bihar. By then, too, he had also established himself as a literary figure in the region and become friends with several reputed writers—including Kashinath Singh. I had once casually asked him if he could arrange a meeting with Kashinath

Singh, and he said that he would keep my request in mind.

And this morning, as I laze in the hotel after breakfast, wondering what my day is going to look like, I get a call from Ramdeo Singh. He knows I am in Banaras and informs me that he too is in town and is meeting Kashinath Singh in the evening—and that I should come along.

'These days he likes to take a nap in the afternoon, so he has asked us to come at five,' Ramdeo Singh tells me. 'I have briefed him about you.'

Kashinath Singh, the author of *Kashi ka Assi*, which has been reissued fourteen times and sold over 30,000 copies; a writer who has won many laurels including the Sahitya Akademi Award; the younger brother of Namvar Singh, another literary great—until a few moments ago he had seemed remote and out of my reach. And now, I have secured an appointment with him, without turning a single stone. If this is not a miracle, then what is?

35.

KASHINATH SINGH LIVES in a colony not very far from Assi. The autorickshaw drivers, it turns out, are on strike. They have parked their vehicles at Godowlia and are standing in a huddle.

'If I take you,' one driver tells us, 'other autorickshaw drivers down the road are going to smash my screen.'

He remains unmoved even after I offer him a handsome amount, but relents when I tell him that our destination is Kashinath Singh's home. He even offers—in return for some extra money—to wait for us till we finish our meeting and bring us back to Godowlia.

As we make our way through the evening traffic, Ramdeo Singh tells me about life in the village. I should be paying attention because his stories are worth recording, but my mind is numbed with anxiety. Banarasis, as I know by now, are dismissive of those trying to understand Banaras, and Kashinath Singh is one man who understands Banaras better than most: what if he doesn't find me worthy of his time and attention? What's nagging me even more is that I still can't think of questions intelligent enough to put to a literary figure of his stature.

Kashinath Singh answers the doorbell himself. His beard looks his age, which is a little over eighty, but his eyes belong to a child who has just committed a prank and is waiting for its outcome. He and his wife live alone in Banaras: one of their two sons is posted in Tokyo and the other in Pondicherry.

'Before you ask me anything,' Kashinath Singh fixes his gaze on me, 'let me ask you what you make of Banaras.'

Caught unawares, I begin to ramble. He listens to me attentively. When I finally tell him that I found people of Banaras to be wise because they seemed to be acutely aware that nothing in life is permanent, he begins to speak.

'You are absolutely right,' he says. 'People here regard attachment and detachment equally. They look happy and carefree, as if they have unravelled the mystery of life. If a man wearing nothing but a gamchha runs into a wealthy, well-dressed man, he does not feel inferior in any way. He remains just as happy.

'But of late that Banaras has been changing. Earlier it used to be a city of mohallas, now it is a city of colonies. Earlier, the neighbour played a great role in your life. For example, if your neighbour spotted your child smoking, he would consider it his duty to inform you—he would even take the liberty of slapping the child to discipline him. But now, if you slapped your neighbour's child, there would be trouble.

'One more thing—a very important thing—is fast disappearing from Banaras: laughter. People were in the habit of laughing out loudly, it came naturally to them.

'There is a story in *Kashi ka Assi*, you must have noticed, titled *Kaun Thagwa Nagariya Lootal Ho* (which conman robbed our city). Nagar, the city, is the human body and soul. The *thagwa*, conman, represents our problems. The story is about laughter disappearing from our daily lives—so much so that people began turning to TV for their dose of humour—but there is one man who still retains the capability of laughing out loud, and he has left home after a tiff with his family. Intelligence agencies begin a frantic search for him because the man is a rarity—the only one who can still laugh—and they want to place him in the museum.

'Banaras used to be like that man. People would laugh out loud, without any worry, without any hesitation, irrespective of whether they had eaten or were starving. That trait is fast disappearing. Laughter used to be the essence of Banaras. Now you have schools that teach you how to smile.'

His wife, Kusum, serves us tea and peda. The peda has come from Ramnagar.

'When did you first come to Banaras?' I ask him.

'I was born in 1937, in a village called Jiyanpur'—not very far from Banaras—'and I finished high school there. In 1953, my elder brother Namvar Singh, you must have heard about him, brought me to Banaras for further studies. He was already teaching here.

'We lived at Assi, in a Brahmin mohalla called Lolark Kund. The kund (pond) was quite famous because it was believed that if a childless woman bathed in it, she would become a mother. There would be more watchers than bathers. I think Tulsidas had cursed Brahmins—he himself was a Brahmin who had been troubled by other Brahmins—that is why no one in the neighbourhood seemed to have a job. They would all leave home in the morning, looking to be hired to conduct religious rituals.

'I think my elder brother was the only one in the neighbourhood who had a formal education and held a regular job. And I was the only boy who went to school to study earnestly. Other boys came to school only to eat the free porridge that was served. Do you eat paan?'

'I don't.'

'If you permit me, may I have one?'

'Please go ahead.'

'After finishing school I joined BHU. I finished my MA in 1959 and PhD in 1963, and joined BHU as a lecturer in 1965. I had already started writing by 1960. I was influenced by Ernest Hemingway, Tolstoy, Gorky, Turgenev. Later, I also read Samuel Beckett, Jean Paul Sartre, Albert Camus, Franz Kafka. I think all the Hindi writers of my time read Sartre, Camus and Kafka.

'In 1968, a collection of my stories came out as a book for the first time. One of the stories in it, which was later translated into many languages—in English it was titled *Bliss*—had already established my reputation as a writer. It is about a just-retired postal employee who, as he is whiling away his time at home, happens to watch the sun set. He finds the sun to be absolutely red, and in its fading light, even his kurta and the wall behind him have turned red. He is so overcome by the sight that he calls out to his wife, his grandchildren, even passersby, asking them to watch the spectacle. He wants to share his joy with them. But they laugh at him. They tell him, "This may be new to you, we watch it every day." He bursts into tears. He realises that all his working life he had never had the time to enjoy a sunset.'

'Did you use the redness of the sun to convey your communist leanings?' Ramdeo Singh asks him.

'No, I had no such thought at the time,' replies Kashinath Singh.

'How did *Kashi ka Assi* come about?' I ask him.

'The stories in it were inspired by the conversations I would overhear at Pappu's chai shop in Assi. When I began working on the stories, in the late 1980s, Banaras was a democratic place. By the time the anthology was published, in 2002, Banaras had ceased to be democratic. Now, democracy is shaky in the entire country. There is no respect for the Constitution, there is hardly any freedom of speech.

'In the same Banaras, a few hundred years ago, different schools of thought coexisted. We had Kabir, who was a Muslim; we had Ravidas, who was a Dalit; we had Tulsidas, who was a Brahmin. Banaras gave space to all.'

'How often would you visit Pappu's teashop?' I ask him.

'He would walk to the shop every evening,' his wife replies. 'He went there for months. He would return home late in the night. Back then he was still teaching in BHU; we lived on the campus. We moved to this house only in 1997, when he retired.'

'Did he ever show you his work before sending it for publication?' I ask her.

'Once in a while, I would look at a page lying open. I hardly had the time. I was too busy with household chores and bringing up the kids.'

'Your name means the Lord of Kashi,' I tell Kashinath Singh, 'but I gather you don't believe in God.'

'I was in school when I last went inside Vishwanath Temple, along with my father. After that I have only accompanied friends till the outside—I never went in. Whenever my father stayed in Banaras, he would visit the Sankat Mochan Temple every morning. I would accompany him but never step inside the temple. I don't believe in God, but I don't interfere with other people's faiths. My father would bathe in the Ganga every morning; I would accompany him but not step into the water.'

'But you used to bathe in the Ganga in your younger days,' the wife reminds him, 'you would even swim in it.'

'I did that for fun,' Kashinath Singh replies, 'I didn't do that out of faith.'

'Do you believe in God?' I ask the wife.

'Yes, I am quite religious.'

'Were you ever embarrassed about the bad words he has used in *Kashi ka Assi*? Did you admonish him?'

She evades a reply and simply smiles. Then she says, 'But I was embarrassed when I heard those abusive words in the movie. Even women are shown using such words. In real life women don't speak like that. They don't speak like that even in the novel.'

'By the way, how did you people get here?' Kashinath Singh asks us.

'We took an autorickshaw.'

'Is the driver waiting?'

'Yes.'

'Kusum,' he tells his wife, 'why don't you give the driver some tea. It's quite cold outside.'

'Does the thought ever cross your mind,' I ask him, 'that you might have been more popular as a writer had you written in English?'

'I never thought that way. Most Hindi writers write for college libraries, for teachers and students of literature, for critics. My readers, on the other hand, are not just literature students. My readers also include those who have studied medicine, sociology, commerce, computer science, and so on. I am one of the more popular Hindi writers today. Of course, I am nowhere close to the popular names that write in English. Writing is their occupation. For me writing has never been an occupation, I had a job and now I get pension. Writing has been my passion.'

'How difficult would it have been to make a living as a writer had you not had the job with BHU?'

'There have been quite a few writers who made a living out of writing. There was Premchand, who initially had a job but gave it up to devote himself to writing. The other names that come to my mind are Yashpal and Jainendra Kumar. I think even Phanishwar Nath Renu didn't have a regular job. Rajendra Yadav too was a full-time writer. These people took writing seriously.'

'So did you.'

'In my case, well, let me quote a couplet: "*Sirf hone se kuchh nahin hota, hone ka haq adaa kijiye*" (It's not enough to just exist, you have to justify your existence).'

'Would you have become a writer if you lived outside Banaras?'

'I wouldn't have been able to do the kind of writing I have done. In Banaras, literature has always been people-oriented; it has always been connected to the grassroots. You get plenty of material, even when you are sleeping on the ghats. This is a city that barely sleeps, people are out till one in the night, and you see them again from three in the morning. When I was with the Naxal movement, I would be out on the streets sticking posters in the wee hours, and I would still see people about.'

'You were a part of the Naxal movement?'

'Yes.'

'Were you married by then?'

'We got married in 1962,' his wife replies. 'The Naxal movement began in the late '60s. He grew involved in the early '70s.'

'But I got disenchanted very quickly,' says Kashinath Singh. 'Once, they held a coordination committee meeting somewhere near Asansol in Bengal. Representatives from all states had come. We were all put up in the bungalow of an engineer, and there the representatives were delighted to find a bathtub. They would linger in it for hours, soaping themselves. That was a big disappointment for me, to find people enjoying themselves in the bathtub. I asked myself: "Is this what the struggle all about?"

'There was another reason why I quit. Since I had a job in the university—a government job—some of the comrades would regard me with suspicion. They thought I might betray them. I would let them use my house for meetings, serve them tea, pay for posters and pamphlets, still they didn't trust me entirely. I thought, then, that I should stick to writing.'

'What time of the day do you write? Are you working on anything at the moment?'

'No, I am not writing anything now. Spondylitis is troubling me. Most of my writing has been done after dinner. I would rest my back on the sofa or bed, draw my knees up and place the writing pad on the knees. I would write till six in the morning.'

I place a copy of *Kashi ka Assi* in front of him and hand him my pen. When I had purchased the book three years ago, I had not imagined it would get autographed someday.

'Oh, a fountain pen!' He examines my Mont Blanc. 'Anyone who uses a fountain pen is worth remembering. I can't think of any writer who still uses a fountain pen—except Doodhnath Singh.'

I don't ask him who Doodhnath Singh is.

'If you don't mind, will you drop me at the paan shop?' he asks.

'By all means,' I reply. 'We will drop you back home too.'

'No, I will walk back.' He asks his wife for twenty rupees, and then the three of us get into the autorickshaw.

Kashinath Singh gets down at the paan shop and takes leave with a namaste so earnest as if I had done him a great favour by meeting him. This time his eyes don't look mischievous, but very fatherly.

Only after we drop him off at the paan shop does Ramdeo Singh reveal to me that Kashinath Singh had actually cancelled an engagement in order to have me over. He was supposed to have been at Assi this evening as the chief guest at the staging of Kalidasa's drama *Abhigyan Shakuntala*. Since the play was going to be staged on two consecutive days, he had told the organisers that he would be attending it the next day.

'Can I go along too?' I ask Ramdeo Singh.

'I will ask him.'

36.

THE NEXT MORNING Ramdeo Singh calls me to say that Kashinath Singh would allow me to come to the play on the condition that I have dinner with him after the event.

I decide not to walk the ghats and galis today and preserve my energies for the evening. But why waste a beautiful day staring at the phone or the walls of my hotel room? I set out for Dashashwamedha intending to take a boat ride to the opposite bank and back.

'Massage, sir?'

Even before I can reply, the young masseur is kneading my upper arm to demonstrate his skills.

Before long, I am lying face down on one of the countless cots at Dashashwamedha, sharing it with a priest conducting business with a client. What would Banaras be without the cots, the parasols, the priests, the pilgrims, the masseurs, the boatmen? It wouldn't be Banaras at all.

The masseur is walking on my back, energising my vertebrae with the balls of his feet. He is holding on to the parasol to ensure his entire weight isn't on me. The relief is even greater when he walks on my lower back and butt. All the pain accumulated from the long walks melts away. It's a far better sensation than washing away your sins in the river, although I don't know how it feels doing that. But how convenient: you commit a sin and then wash it away. End of guilt.

I remember the long taxi ride I had once taken in Hyderabad, from my hotel to the airport. The driver, a middle-aged Muslim, gave me a detailed account of the rich sex life he had had, which included sleeping with Arab women when he worked in Saudi Arabia. Then, one day, he went to Mecca and rid himself of all his sins. He returned to Hyderabad a pure man, richer by memories and a lot more money.

Rejuvenated, I step into the boat. The river turns out to be a riot of migratory birds. From the ghat they are just a pretty sight, but once on the boat, you feel their ferocity, the collective flapping of wings.

The larger the number of people in a boat, the greater is the number of birds encircling it, looking for food. Since my hands are empty, the birds leave me alone. When the boatman calls out, 'Aah, aah, aah', some of them come flying towards us, but once they assess we have nothing to offer, fly away.

The opposite bank has a large number of bathers too. As I get closer I notice that a family is recording its visit to Banaras: a middle-aged couple, the woman in a bright red sari and the man in Amul underwear, standing in thigh-deep water. Their palms are joined in a namaste. They are posing for a young man, presumably their son, who is perched on a boat. I wonder how the pictures are going to come out because the sun is behind the couple. If the couple turned around and the boy clicked those pictures from the sands, the result would be spectacular: a sun-bathed couple posing against the expanse of Banaras.

I buy tea from a makeshift stall and wonder whether bathing on this side of the Ganga cleanses one of sins as effectively as it does on the ghats of Banaras. Ideally, it should. It's the same stretch of river—*uttar-vahini*—north-bound, kissed by the first rays of the sun. But there is a vital difference. When you step into the water in Banaras, you face both, the river and the rising sun; whereas on this side, one of these powerful elements will be staring at your wet bum. Which is why, Banaras is Banaras.

In the evening, I reach Assi well before time. The play will be staged at the open-air theatre, where yoga classes and music concerts are conducted in the mornings. It is open to the public—one didn't need permission—but it would inflate my importance to be seen as Kashinath Singh's guest.

Ramdeo Singh is already there. He is talking to a stocky, bald man who is dressed in a kurta and loose pajamas and has a neatly-folded shawl hanging from his shoulders.

'Meet Dr Gaya Singh,' Ramdeo Singh introduces him to me, 'he is a former principal of Harishchandra College and the only character in *Kashi ka Assi* whose original name has been retained.'

Gaya Singh bursts out laughing. In this part of the country his laughter would be called a *thahaka*, the loud spontaneous kind that can be heard miles away, the kind that, according to one of Kashinath Singh's stories, is fast disappearing. It must indeed be disappearing because I have heard someone laugh like this after a long, long time.

Gaya Singh: of course I remember this character from *Kashi ka Assi*, a buffoonish but headstrong man who has a taste for challenging authority. The Gaya Singh portrayed in *Mohalla Assi* looks and talks more like a Punjabi, but the real Gaya Singh is a typical Banarasi. You can't get more typical than that—the attire, the accent, the laughter.

Soon, Kashinath Singh and his wife arrive. I greet them and quietly take a seat two rows behind them. The front row is reserved for the distinguished people of Banaras.

'When I looked at the sky a moment ago,' the vivacious emcee begins, 'I found not a single star. But who needs those stars when I see so many stars right in front me.'

She names the stars—the distinguished guests—and requests them to come onto the stage. They line up, Kashinath Singh at the centre. Each one is expected to say a few words. Kashinath Singh begins, 'The well-known journalist and writer'—I hear my name—'happens to be in our midst. It would only be appropriate to have him on stage as well.'

I join the galaxy, and when my turn comes, I say something to the effect that it has been a long journey for me: from cremating my mother at Manikarnika, to sharing the stage with the distinguished people of Banaras at Assi. People clap.

After the show, several members of the cast—all young men and women, still wearing their costumes—encircle Kashinath Singh to seek his blessings. That's the true test of how good a writer you are, when the popularity of your book or books transcends generations. A book that remains in print in spite of changing times and tastes is no longer a book but a classic. *Kashi ka Assi* is one such.

Even as I regard the scene from a distance, two men come up to me and introduce themselves. They are both doctors from Banaras and one of them, it turns out, has read *Chai, Chai*. It occurs to me that it has been many years since I travelled for the book, and now the book is doing the travelling.

I join Kashinath Singh, his wife and Ramdeo Singh as they walk towards a nearby restaurant for dinner. We are led by Gaya Singh who, being a distinguished resident of Assi, is our host tonight.

Assi, I notice, now has a Zumba studio and some new boutiques and cafés as well. They have all shut for the day. The restaurant, however, is open and the manager, very respectfully, shows us to a comfortable corner.

'If you permit me,' Kashinath Singh tells me, 'I would like to hand over this shawl to you.' He had been welcomed to the stage with the white shawl. I accept it without hesitation.

I mention to him that I found it heartening to see him being surrounded by young admirers.

He laughs. 'Writers in Banaras have generally been neglected during their lifetime,' he says. 'Take Tulsidas, for example. Then Jaishankar Prasad, such a great writer. He too was from Banaras. He died in 1937, not even fifty years old. His *Kamayani* is probably the best work in Hindi literature after the *Ramcharitmanas*. Once, he was reading out from one of his works at a function when a mischievous element in the audience threw a lizard on the dais.

'When Munshi Premchand, another Banarasi, died in 1936, there were barely fifteen people in his funeral procession. One man watching the procession asked another: "Who died?" The reply was, "*Koi master guzar gaya hai*"—some teacher has passed away.'

'That's also true of many writers such as Kafka,' I tell him, 'who became famous posthumously.'

'You are right, even George Orwell.'

Hot rotis are served along with dal and curries. Gaya Singh urges us to eat well.

I ask Kashinath Singh if his elder brother—Namwar Singh—played a role in his becoming a writer.

'My brother was always critical of me,' he says. 'He would never praise what I had written, but always point out what I *could* have written. In a way, that helped me. He began taking me seriously only after I published my autobiography, *Yaad Ho ki Na Ho*. It was written in the style of a story. The approach was new at the time.'

After dinner, we all walk to a paan shop that sits right next to Pappu's teashop. The teashop is shut for the day. As Kashinath Singh supervises the making of their paan, I take pictures. The idea is to record the writer revisiting his old haunt—his subject.

The car assigned to him arrives and he and his wife leave. I say goodbye to Gaya Singh and tell him I would like to meet him someday to know his own story. Assi, now silent, reverberates with his trademark laughter. 'I am at your service,' he grabs my hand and laughs again.

Ramdeo Singh and I get into an autorickshaw and head back to Godowlia.

'When *Kashi ka Assi* was published,' Ramdeo Singh tells me, 'Kashinath Singh was unable to visit Assi for many months. People were angry with him because of the manner they had been portrayed in the book. Gaya Singh was especially angry, not only because of his portrayal but also because his real name had been retained. He didn't talk to Kashinath Singh for a long time.'

'But they seem to be friends now.'

'Yes, people managed to convince him that any publicity is good. He realised that *Kashi ka Assi* had made him famous. They became friends again. A very nice man—this Gaya Singh. When he was not on talking terms with Kashinath Singh, I had stopped talking to him in retaliation. After all, I consider Kashinath Singh as one of my mentors. My daughter was getting married at the time and I decided not to invite Gaya Singh. But he got to know and called me. He rebuked me: "Your daughter is getting married and you haven't invited me?" I was embarrassed, and I told him I would send an invitation card right away. He said, "I don't need an invitation card to attend your daughter's wedding. I will come." And he actually came. Nice man, very good at heart.'

'Even I think so. Someone who can laugh like that has to be good at heart.'

'Today, Assi has great respect for Kashinath Singh. They even celebrate his birthday every year, on January 1, at Pappu's teashop. He doesn't attend, but they still celebrate it.'

I infer that both Kashinath Singh and Assi have made each other famous beyond their known circles.

It is past eleven when I get dropped off at Godowlia, but the place is just as lively as it had been some hours ago. Craving for some more dessert, I step into a sweet shop opposite my hotel for some hot rasgullas. It is a nameless shop—some of the best eating joints are nameless—and I have been visiting it regularly ever since I was told by the shopkeeper that no sweet on display is older than six hours.

As I finish eating and step out of the shop, I find two men waiting for me. They are the two doctors I had just met at Assi. They were passing by on a scooter and had stopped on noticing me inside. This time, we have an extended chat. The one who has read my book is Dr Kartikeya Singh, the other is Dr Sanjay Rai.

They tell me that after watching the play, they had gone to Tulsi Ghat to meet 'Mahant ji' and were now headed home.

Mahant is a title enjoyed by the head of a temple or religious order, and the administration of the temples built by Tulsidas is now run by a family that has had the job handed down by their ancestors. The responsibility currently rests with Vishwambhar Nath Mishra, a professor of electronics engineering at the BHU. His younger brother, Dr Vijay Nath Mishra, is a reputed neurosurgeon who has served as the head of the neurology department at the Institute of Medical Sciences in BHU.

Their father, Veer Bhadra Mishra, who had become the mahant of the Tulsidas temples at the age of fourteen, and held the job until he died in 2013, when he was seventy-four, was a hydraulic engineer by qualification and had served as the head of the civil engineering department at the BHU. In 1999, *Time* magazine had featured him as one of their 'Heroes for the Planet' because of his efforts to clean the Ganga.

All highly respected men of science, but at the same time revered as men of God. This, too, is Banaras.

I ask the two doctors whether it would be possible for me to meet the mahant sometime. 'That can be arranged,' says Dr Sanjay Rai, who is the more expressive of the two. I notice that he has stone-studded rings on all his fingers and multiple chains and rudraksha necklaces around his neck. On his forehead is a saffron smudge. He could pass for a living example of superstition—or belief, if you like—but he is actually a qualified doctor, an MD at that, and, as I learn, also the son of a reputed paediatrician in Banaras. His mother-in-law, too, is a reputed doctor, and his wife a dentist.

Doctors know the human body inside out; they get to see our organs, something that we never do even though they belong to us; they are able to tell how healthy or ill we are; they often extend our lifespan by treating us—they could be God. Why, then, does a doctor believe in God?

The answer, in my opinion, lies in the uncertainty.

That anyone who is born is going to die is a certainty, but when exactly one is going to die—not even the most accomplished of doctors can predict. People who've just had a successful heart surgery can die the very next day, whereas those given six months to live can go on to live for a further six years. Then there is always the possibility of accidents, of all kinds, which can happen to anyone, anytime—no doctor can predict or prevent them.

This unpredictability of life keeps God alive. That is why even doctors fear God. They too are humans, only that they understand the functioning of the human body better than others. When, in spite of their expertise, they get to witness the unexplained all the time—a healthy man dying and the dying going on to live—they perhaps appreciate God and planetary movements more.

I would still like to know from Dr Sanjay Rai why the hand that writes prescriptions should wear so many rings. I invite him to have breakfast with me the next morning.

37.

THE GALIS OF Banaras are great levellers. Since they are too narrow for cars, the rich as well as the poor either use two-wheelers or just walk through them. In which other city can you imagine two doctors—both highly qualified, mid-career and hailing from prosperous families—roaming on a scooter without giving a damn what people think? Those who know them know who they are. Those who don't know them—how does their opinion matter?

Dr Sanjay Rai is parking his scooter when I go down to receive him. He apologises for being late. He had had an unexpected patient, who was not only unwell but had also lost his wallet. The doctor wrote him a prescription and also gave him sufficient money to buy the medicines and meet travel expenses.

Once we settle for breakfast at a table overlooking Godowlia, Dr Rai tells me: 'We aren't originally from Banaras, our village is in Azamgarh. My father—Dr B.B. Rai, who is a well-known paediatrician in Banaras—was in government service. From 1967 to '72, he was posted in Lucknow as the personal physician of the governor of Uttar Pradesh, B. Gopala Reddy. In 1972, when the Governor's term was coming to an end, he asked my father where he would like to be posted. My father, who was thirty-three at the time, chose Banaras.

'He chose Banaras because it was close to Azamgarh, where his village was located, and also close to Ghazipur, where my mother's village was located. By then, the medical college at BHU had opened and people from Azamgarh and Ghazipur already came to Banaras for treatment. He thought this was a better place to be.

'I was seven when we moved to Banaras. After I finished school, I joined BSc at BHU and, because I wanted to be a doctor, also joined coaching classes to get into a medical college. I had just finished my BSc when I finally got through the medical entrance, and as luck would have it, got a seat in BHU.

'I completed my MBBS, MD—all from Banaras. I applied for a government job and in the meantime worked at the hospital in Ramakrishna Mission. In 2001, I got the job and my first posting was in Jaunpur, another neighbouring district. Once again visited by good fortune, the village I was posted to was located on the border of Banaras and Jaunpur, so I didn't have to shift to Jaunpur. I would travel to the village every day. In 2004, I got a formal transfer to Banaras and I have been posted here ever since.'

'People like moving to bigger cities for better prospects. What made you stay in Banaras?'

'The thing was, my wife's family was also from Banaras. We were neighbours. When I was studying for MBBS, the dean and director of the medical college was a lady called Priyamvada Tiwari, a well-known gynaecologist. She took a liking to me and decided that I should marry her daughter. She went to my father with a proposal. I got married in 1994, when I was still in the first year of MD. The next year, my first daughter was born. I have two daughters.

'My wife, when she finished her course in dentistry, set up private practice. She wanted to devote equal time to practice and family. She didn't want a government job because she had seen how busy her mother had been throughout her career. Once she set up a clinic here, there was no question of my leaving Banaras. The city turned out to be a magnet to me. It has kept me stuck to it, and I like it that way.'

'You are a doctor—why do you believe so much in God?'

'True, I am a doctor. I have seen children being born. I have seen people dying. I know how the human body functions. But, *kuchh to hai*—there is something. There is an unexplained, unseen force. Why do some smokers live till as late as ninety, whereas some non-smokers die much younger of lung cancer? Why do some alcoholics live long whereas some non-drinkers die of liver problems? How do you explain these things?

'You also tend to inherit your faith and religious customs from your family. Moreover, Banaras is a spiritual city. That, too, is a huge influence. Way back, when I was doing my BSc, I would walk to college and the Sankat Mochan Temple was on my way. Initially, I would stop at the temple only occasionally and then it became a habit. Since devotees of Lord Hanuman fast on Tuesdays, I too started fasting on Tuesdays. It became so much a part of my life that it no longer mattered why I fast on Tuesdays.

'For the past one year, I have also been fasting on Sundays. A friend advised me to do that and I don't regret it. In fact, I have begun to enjoy fasting. Your body is rid of toxins and you feel lighter. Not only that, you feel spiritually strong.

'Last year, my father had a heart attack, he underwent surgery and had a stent installed. But he went into congestive heart failure shortly after that. The doctor who had performed the surgery was not available. I am a doctor, but there was hardly anything I could do except be by my father's side in the ICU. That's when I prayed, and my father recovered. He is almost eighty, but he has resumed his practice. If you come home you will see sixty to seventy patients waiting for their turn to be seen. So, there is indeed God.'

I ask Dr Rai about the rings he wears. Each one turns out to have a story behind it. One was recommended by the family priest, another was given to him by his father on the advice of an astrologer, yet another was given to him by his mother when he was studying to get into a medical college. A couple of them have been given by his wife, for good luck. Then there is one gifted to him by his mother-in-law. And so on. Similar are the stories behind the many chains he wears.

'Have these rings influenced your life in any way?' I ask him.

'I never went looking for these rings. They were all given to me at different times—they kept adding up. But yes, sometimes I do feel they have a positive effect on me. Since things have been going fine for me, I would like to believe they have a role to play.'

'What do you like about Banaras?'

'Banaras is a city of masti—fun. It is a happy-go-lucky city. In other cities, neighbours hardly know one another, but here everybody knows everybody else. The rich don't look down upon the poor, the poor don't look at the rich with awe. Each one is happy the way he is.

'Every single—I repeat, every *single*—circle of friends will include people who are rich as well as those who don't count as rich—that's the specialty of Banaras. A professor can be friends with a shopkeeper, a doctor can be friends with a priest, there is no distinction—unlike in bigger cities where professors only mingle with professors and doctors mingle only with other doctors.

'If you have lost your way somewhere and ask for directions, people will go out of their way to tell you how to get there. Sometimes, if your destination is nearby, they will even accompany you to make sure you reach it. How can one not like a place like this?

'It so happens that both my daughters are also studying in BHU. The elder one was keen to do her post-graduation in Delhi and even made a round of colleges there, but, for some reason, she changed her mind and decided to continue her studies in Banaras. She is very attached to her grandfather—my father. The younger one too wanted to study in Delhi but eventually took admission in BHU.

'Tomorrow they may move to other cities, who knows? But right now the entire family is in Banaras. What more can I ask for? Both, Lord Vishwanath and Sankat Mochan, have been very kind to me.'

After breakfast, I sit behind Dr Rai on his scooter and we head for Chowk, the oldest and busiest market area of the city. It is not very far from Godowlia. This is where mainly weavers congregate—to hand over their products to wholesalers.

Dr Rai, however, is taking me to meet not a weaver but a priest, whose family has been associated with the Vishwanath Temple. He thinks I might get some material to write about.

The priest, Deepak Malaviya, turns out to be an imposing man, his voice intimidating. He is busy dictating a horoscope to his son, who is seated at another desk, typing the predictions on a computer. What they are preparing is the astrological equivalent of a pathologist's report, which will tell the client whether planetary positions are in his favour and, if not, the precautionary or corrective measures he must take.

The horoscope—kundli—is a crucial document. Even a bleak report from the pathologist can be attributed to the horoscope: 'He was destined to fall ill during this phase of his life.' The horoscope makes marriages; and if those break, the blame falls on mismatched birth charts. It makes people choose professions and change locations. It helps them pick the auspicious time for worldly endeavours. It is, in essence, the roadmap of life.

I wonder if Malaviya is irritated by the intrusion, but feel at ease when he tells Dr Rai, 'I am so glad you came, it saves me the trouble of going all the way to your place to hand over this invitation. My son is getting married next month, please come with your family.'

Both Dr Rai and I congratulate the son, who acknowledges our greetings with a shy smile. His hand, which has now stopped typing, plucks an invitation from a stack and on the envelope he writes out Dr Rai's name, carefully suffixing it with 'and family'. He then passes on the invitation to his father, who stands up and respectfully hands it over to Dr Rai.

Black tea is ordered from a nearby stall. I tell Malaviya about my mother's cremation at Manikarnika—by now I have realised this is the easiest way to strike a chord with a Banarasi—and learn anew how Banaras is so accepting of death.

He tells me: 'The ancient texts about Kashi say, *"Maranam mangalam yatro"*, which means "Death is auspicious." Anywhere else in the world, death is considered inauspicious, but not here. About Kashi it is also said, *"Kashiyam maranam mukti"*, which means if you die in Kashi, you are liberated.

'In other places, a dead body is considered impure. If you happen to touch a dead body, you go home and bathe. But in Kashi, it is not uncommon for people to brush past a body. They place a hand on their heads and say *"Har Har Mahadev"* and move on. *Yahaan, shav bhi Shankar hai* (here, even a dead body is considered to be Shiva).'

'How did you come into this line?'

'This is our family business. We have been priests for generations. My son is the fifth generation. My father was not so much into astrology; he and his ancestors were mainly into karmakand—conducting rituals for important events in life, such as birth, death, marriage, and so on. I decided to diversify into astrology.

'When I asked my son if he would like to follow my profession, he said yes. He has studied in St John's, one of the best convents in Banaras; he has even done his MCom. He is also an acharya in astrology. He is studying towards his post-graduation in astrology, and in four months, will enrol for a doctorate.

'People like us are always in great demand, and of late even our fortunes have changed along with those of our clients. I have conducted weddings in at least ten countries: America, Singapore, Malaysia, Indonesia, Thailand, Nepal, and many more. There is a wedding coming up in Scotland.

'We don't have the means to fly to America and stay in posh hotels in places like Washington and San

Fransisco. Such good fortune comes to us only because of our clients. When I was a student myself—I studied BA in political science from BHU—I used to wonder whether karmakand had a future in the changing times. But my father advised me to stay focused on it, despite the fact that he remained quite poor all his life.

'I was born into poverty and deprivation. Back during my father's time, clients rarely paid him in cash. They would bring a kilo of fruits or five kilos of rice—things like that. Today, people like us are more in demand than ever. And there is a lot of cash. In hindsight, my father was right in asking me to stick to the family business.

'Clients now come from all over the place, as I told you. Someone has a wedding in California, someone in Goa—they want us to conduct the rituals. We tell them to give us flight tickets and they are only too happy to oblige. Business in Banaras is in the hands of the Marwari community, and the priests engaged by them are invariably from my family.

'You see, there are two kinds of Brahmins in Banaras. One is the illiterate kind, who goes door to door with Ganga water, offering his blessings or services. Some people give him a rupee or two, others tell him "*aagey badho*"—move on. Then there are Brahmins—people like us—who have a good command over their field and therefore command great respect. In no other profession do you get such respect.

'In order to retain that respect we must periodically keep going back to the ancient texts. If you don't chant a set of mantras for a month you tend to forget them, so you must keep memorising them. The layman may not know whether the mantra you are chanting is related to marriage or birth or death, but there might be someone in the audience who catches on, therefore we can't afford to make fools of ourselves. Whenever we find free time, we practise the chants, sometimes for five to six hours at a stretch. There are several occasions—like yagnas—when the priest has the mike in hand for eight to ten hours, and is watched by hundreds of people. He cannot afford to go wrong.'

'There are twelve primary Shiva temples across the country—what's special about the Vishwanath Temple?' I ask.

'The peace you find at Vishwanath Temple is incomparable. Have you seen the shine of the lingam? It glows like no other. And when you touch the lingam, you are filled with bliss.'

'I too have touched it,' I say, 'but they didn't let me touch it for more than a second.'

'There is a reason behind that,' Malaviya says. 'If a person who is pure in thought and action touches it for a long time, then there is no problem. But if a sinner happens to prolong his touch, he experiences—this is what I have been told—something like an electric shock. That is why they don't let anyone touch the lingam for long.

'In my case, if I don't visit the temple and touch the lingam periodically, I begin to feel disturbed. The moment I touch it, I am overcome by a beautiful sensation I cannot describe in words. The only other Shiva temple where I have experienced a similar sensation was at the Mahakal temple in Ujjain.'

'Considering you are so busy, can I assume that more people believe in astrology these days?' I ask him.

'You have no idea how many people come to me. Those who claim in the morning that they don't believe in astrology come to me quietly in the evening, saying, "Panditji, please take a look at my horoscope." You should not run too much behind astrology, it is a science that gives you an idea of what could be in store for you. It does not mean good things will come to you without your lifting a finger. *Karm pradhan hai*—action is the key.'

'You seem to be the first astrologer to say so.'

'Astrology may be my source of income, but I have absolute dislike for people who come to me thrice a week to show me their horoscopes. I tell them, "Don't run blindly after astrology, you have to do your work as well."'

38.

'DO YOU CONSIDER yourself a man of science or a man of God?' I ask Vishwambhar Nath Mishra when I get to meet him in the evening at his office on Tulsi Ghat.

As far as looks go, Mishra can pass for a distinguished Hindi-belt politician who has seen many elections: he is clad in a white kurta-pajama and a black waistcoat, and sports thick grey hair and a toothbrush moustache. He is only fifty-three, but is one of the most revered figures of Banaras: a professor of electronics engineering who is also the custodian of the temples established by Tulsidas. People flock to him for advice.

He is in a hurry at the moment. He has to attend a couple of weddings. He was, in fact, preparing to leave when I entered his office but has now resettled in his couch to answer my question.

'I was born in a spiritual family,' Mishra replies, 'so spiritualism is inbuilt in me. Science has given me the vision to take a closer look at my religion. In a modern society, you cannot survive if you are not updated with scientific developments. But at the same time, when people come to me with their problems, I direct them to the religious text that is considered the ultimate work of literature, the *Ramcharitmanas*.

'One can't be sure of what all was going through Tulsidas's mind when he composed it, but in the text there is a lot to be read between the lines. And a man of science can better appreciate what's between the lines than someone not familiar with science. *Ramcharitmanas* is the biggest key to life. Even today, scholars are researching it.'

'Why do people pray to God when they know death is one day certain and can happen anytime?' I ask him.

'Death is certain, that's true. But before death there is life. If people are going to temples, it means prayers are working for them—why else would they go? Take the case of River Ganga. She gives you both, bhukti and mukti—food and liberation. While you are alive, she provides you with food, but when you are dying, she promises you liberation.

'Who are we? We are a part and parcel of almighty God. He has sent us here in the physical form. Our body does not belong to us. It belongs to the five elements and has to go back to them. And as for your soul, it is liberated by Kashi, by Lord Vishwanath and the Ganga. Together they free you from the circle of life and death.

'If you happen to die in Kashi, liberation is guaranteed. That is why even death is celebrated here. The same can't be said about those who die elsewhere but are cremated in Kashi. As long as you live in Kashi, you are a part of Shiva. You are here only because he has willed you to be here. How long you are going to stay here, he decides. If he doesn't want you to be a part of him, he can drive you out in a minute.'

'Let me rephrase my original question,' I tell him. 'While I was in the other room waiting to see you, I happened to notice a bunch of invitations received by your office. Some of them address you as "Professor" and some others as "Mahant". Which of these titles fits you better?'

'It doesn't matter to me what I am addressed as, even though I would prefer the religious title. I am a man of God whose character has been shaped—rather enhanced—by science. My scientific background is a part of my training. You cannot fool me, even in matters to do with God. If you put forth an argument, I can counter you with a better argument.

'See, it is like this. Spiritualism begins where science ends. Let's imagine two surgeons, both equally qualified. While one always gets his surgeries right, the other always messes up—why? It's the hand of God. When a doctor writes a prescription, he is merely being a messenger of God.

'There is usually a conflict between science and spiritualism. Both call each other frauds. But I recommend a combination of both—that way you are safe.'

I walk out of his office a little confused, but at the same time agreeing about one thing he said: that it is safe to have equal faith in doctors and God when you or a dear one is ill. You don't lose anything, do you?

But, I regret having forgotten to ask him one vital question. What happens when an ardent devotee of Shiva, who has never sinned in his life but who doesn't live in Banaras, dies—does he attain liberation or remain deprived of it because his death hasn't taken place in Banaras? By the same logic, does a sinner who has lived and died in Banaras get liberated?

It's too late for me to turn back. The mahant— or professor, if you like—has already left. But I am capable of inventing an answer for myself: the sinner from Banaras will go to heaven because his good deeds in his previous lifetimes in other cities far outweighed the sins he had committed as a Banarasi. That's why God had placed him in Banaras in the first place, so that he could be rewarded.

39.

THE VAST SWEEP of land fed by the Ganga is liberally sprinkled with four-legged wooden stalls that are integral to the culture thriving on these plains. They are the paan shops—if you remove them, you will be taking the flavour out of the culture.

With times changing and the population growing, many of the wooden stalls have transformed into concrete structures, but their role remains unaltered: to supply customers with their daily dose of paan and gossip.

In simpler times and smaller towns, men would dress up in the evenings to stroll to the neighbourhood paan shop to discuss everything, from matters that are public to matters not supposed to be public. The central figure at this congregation would be the man perched on the stall, sitting cross-legged and deftly wrapping paans, his ears absorbing every piece of information.

During the long years I spent in Kanpur—the city where I was born and grew up—I was quite habituated to conversations with people who spoke with their chin upturned so that the paan juice didn't spill out. Paan-chewing is an art. Making a paan is an even higher art—something that Banaras takes pride in. 'Banarasi paan' is a brand, but without copyright. Just about anyone can

Aimless in Banaras

open a shop anywhere in the country and feel free to put 'Banaras' or 'Banarasi' on their signboard.

The number of times I would have had paan in my life would not exceed the number of times I've popped antibiotics. The reason could be that while smoking and drinking were considered cool during the time I was growing up, paan-chewing was always seen as unsophisticated.

And now, after a late lunch, I decide to have a Banarasi paan at a location that can't get more Banarasi: Vishwanath Gali. Before he can begin wrapping my paan, I ask the shopkeeper, whose name is Mohan Lal, what makes Banarasi paan special, and to enlighten me about the art of paan-chewing and paan-making.

He tells me, 'In other places they carelessly apply chuna (slaked lime paste) and kattha (catechu paste) together on the paan—that's not the right way. You should first apply the kattha, and after a few moments, the chuna. Before that, you must wash the paan properly to rid it of all dirt. The kattha should be mixed with itr (scent), and the itr should be chosen according to the season—summer, winter or monsoon.

'The leaf also makes a big difference. We mostly use the Maghai leaf, which begins growing in the month of Magha (mid-January to mid-February) and is available for three months. It is the best betel leaf available. It comes from Gaya.'

'If the leaf comes from Gaya, why should the paan be called Banarasi?' I ask him.

'It is like this. The child is born in Gaya but is brought up in Banaras. The art of seasoning the leaf, the art of wrapping it—these are Banarasi skills. For that matter, nothing comes from Banaras. The betel nut comes from

Assam, the kattha comes from Madhya Pradesh, the itr comes from Kannauj, the tobacco—for those who like to have tobacco—comes from Gujarat. It is all about how you prepare the paan.'

'What's the right way to chew a paan?'

'Once the paan is in your mouth, you should know whether to spit the first lot of juice or swallow it. Ideally, a bit of the first lot of juice generated in the mouth should be spat out, but the second lot should be swallowed—and then you keep swallowing, little by little, while you chew. Many people make eating paan an addiction. They stuff their mouths with one paan after the other and spit wherever they like. They should know where to spit.'

'How does one get to learn this art?'

'How does one learn smoking? You learn by watching others.'

'How long have you been in this business?'

'A very long time. I am seventy-one or seventy-two years old now. My father started this business. I used to help him out as a child. I remember Raj Kapoor coming to this shop, that was more than fifty years ago. Only the other day Rajnath Singh'—India's home minister—'was here. He was standing right where you are standing now.

'Now it is my son, Deepak, who mostly runs the business. I help him out during rush hours. The shop is named after him'—he points to a signboard—'it has been featured in many publications, even *Lonely Planet*.'

I look at the signboard: 'Deepak Tambul Bhandar, Vishwanath Gali, Varanasi.' It's pretty obvious that the shop didn't always have this name: it must have been nameless when Mohan Lal's father set it up, perhaps as a four-legged wooden stall. Now it has acquired not only a name but also fame.

Aimless in Banaras

'Do you also chew paan?' I ask him.

'I do, but not when I am at the shop. I cannot talk to customers with my mouth full.'

Mohan Lal is now joined by Deepak, who is twenty-five years old. Both father and son get busy attending to customers whose number is now swelling by the minute. They are celebrity paanwallahs, after all.

I ask them one last question: what are the scents used for different seasons? But they are pretending not to have heard me.

40.

WANDERING INTO DASHASHWAMEDHA, I spot a familiar face. Is he indeed who I think he is—or a lookalike?

My doubts are dispelled when he waves at me animatedly. He is indeed Debasish Mukherjee, an artist friend about my age, who studied fine arts at BHU a long time ago and now lives in Delhi. He is back—as he is periodically—to rekindle his memories.

Seeing him, I wonder how often I would return once Banaras ceased to be my subject. Would the city be out of my life, having served its purpose, or be weaved even more firmly into my itinerary, having influenced me in more ways than one?

I faced a similar crisis when, living in Chennai, I was working on a book on Calcutta. As long as the book was being written, every moment I spent in Calcutta was potential material. But once the manuscript was sent off to the publisher, what I would see as material became mundane. Yet, the bond I forged with the city during the writing of the book turned out to be so strong that I eventually moved to Calcutta. I have no idea how it is going to be with Banaras—only Shiva knows.

Dashashwamedha is still bathed in sunlight. Another couple of hours before the waving of lights begins. Debasish and I sit on the steps.

'There was no such thing as Ganga Aarti in those days,' he tells me. 'No one felt the need for such over-the-top display of faith in the river. After sunset, the ghats became peaceful.'

'What period are we talking about?' I ask him.

'I studied in BHU from 1990 to 1994. But I guess I am connected to the city through my umbilical cord. My mother was born and brought up here.'

'Really?'

'Yes, I would visit Banaras every summer holiday, from the mid-1970s right through the '80s. My grandmother's house was in Bengali Tola. Back then, Banaras was exactly like the way it is shown in *Joi Baba Felunath*.

'Barely a two-minute walk from her house was Biru-mama's sweet shop. Biru Lal Yadav supplied milk to our family ever since my mother was a little girl. As a child I thought he was part of our extended family. He spoke Bangla fluently. He bought my grandmother's house after she passed away and my maternal uncles moved out of Banaras. In fact, I am coming from the sweet shop right now. I have just learned that Biru mama is no more. I feel sad. I've also had a look at my grandmother's house—it still stands, although 200 years old.

'When I was in BHU, I would cycle from the hostel till here—right where we are sitting—to practice sketching. Once dusk settled over the Ganga, this place looked magical. I would sit for hours together and watch the reflection of lights creating abstract patterns on the Ganga.

'While returning to the hostel, I would sometimes stop by at my grandmother's place. I would weave through the galis of Bengali Tola, past old houses built along the Ganga. The glow of tungsten lights at night would add an amber tone to the aged limestone walls. I am surprised I remember all this so distinctly even after so many years.

'I may have lived in Banaras only for four years, but my stay here remains deeply etched in my mind. Banaras taught me lessons which no book could have ever taught. That period had its share of turbulences. It began with the agitation against the Mandal Commission report and saw the demolition of the Babri mosque in Ayodhya.

'The demolition of the mosque left a scar on me. During the weeks preceding the demolition, Banaras became one of the main centres of right-wing activists. Collecting funds and bricks to build a Ram temple in place of the demolished mosque became a full-time occupation for many. Since the city had seen many riots before, everyone could anticipate what was coming.

'In the beginning of December 1992, as the atmosphere heated up, I moved from the hostel to my grandmother's home. We all were heading for the inevitable. Bengali Tola was adjacent to Madanpura, populated by Muslim weavers. One night, I saw a horrifying sight. Most of our Hindu neighbours had climbed to the rooftops with flaming torches and bells. They were chanting "*Har Har Mahadev*!" That night I discovered that even my cousins were supporters of the right wing.

'This became a regular sight until December 6, when the mosque was pulled down in Ayodhya. Riots broke out in Madanpura and also other parts of Banaras. We remained indoors. News of all kinds kept trickling in from various sources. Many people were killed at a cinema hall near Godowlia. The killings continued for days together. Banaras witnessed the dance of death.

'After remaining holed up in my grandmother's house for a week or so, I decided to leave the city. A curfew was still in force but with some relaxations. One of my cousins organised a boat for me from Pandey Ghat to Rajghat, from where I somehow managed to get an autorickshaw till Mughal Sarai. From Mughal Sarai, I took a train home to Chhapra.

'When I returned to Banaras after a few weeks, Banaras was no longer the same. Earlier, it was common to find Muslims on the ghats. You could see them in large numbers spending the evening by the Ganga. They would linger for hours. They would take boat rides.

'But after the riots, the Muslims stopped coming to the ghats. Occasionally, you would see one or two of them. Their absence changed the look of Banaras—the Banaras I had known.'

41.

AS I HAVE breakfast in the hotel, watching pigeons fly in formation over the Godowlia intersection, I get a call.

'Pranam! This is Gaya Singh.'

'Pranam!'

'Are you going to be at the hotel today?'

'Why, are you coming over?'

'Not right now.' He then explains why he can't come right now. He has just had amla juice to clear his bowels and doesn't consider it safe to venture out for the next few hours because nature might call any time. 'With your permission, can we meet at 12.30?'

'In that case have lunch with me.'

'That would be nice. Pranam!'

As I resume eating, I visualise Gaya Singh pacing up and down in his home, waiting for the pressure to build up in his intestines. I had taken an instant liking to the man when I met him the other night at Assi. He is a trademark Banarasi, who is what he is, nothing affected about him. Such men can come across—and are prone to be easily projected—as comical. It is almost impossible to picture them as sad and reflective; if they are, then something has indeed gone wrong with the world.

Sharp at 12.30 he makes an entry into my room with the dramatic announcement that he has ordered the receptionist to give me a discount. 'The hotel,' he says, 'belongs to a friend. That's the least he can do for me.' He breaks into his signature laughter, which spills out of the open door and reverberates in the corridor.

He is carrying a bunch of hardbound books—all authored by him—for me. They are going to enormously add to my luggage, but no way can I refuse them or, worse, leave them behind. But I do tell him, very honestly, that I am more interested in the contents of his life than of his books. He laughs again.

'Do you eat chicken?' I ask him.

'Why, I eat chicken even on Shivaratri!'

'Great, I will order butter chicken for you.'

Once I place the order, I ask him to tell me his story.

Gaya Singh, his eyes now shut in recollection, tells me: 'I was born in a village called Hingutargarh, not very far from Banaras. Some people back then said I was born in 1948, but I went by what my mother said, that I was born on 4 February 1951. My father was a farmer and an ardent Shiva devotee.

'I studied in the village till Class 12. To the north of the village was a primary school. To the west of the village was a middle school, and to the east of the village, an intermediate school. I did my graduation from a college in Ghazipur. My subjects were Hindi, geography and psychology.'

'Why did you choose psychology?'

'Both geography and psychology are subjects one can put to practical use. After graduation, I went to Calcutta with the idea of doing my post-graduation in geography from there, but after spending a few days in Calcutta I came away. I didn't like that city. One, the water was too salty. Two, I was troubled by the sight of people struggling to make a living—I saw a lot of struggle on the streets. These two things intimidated me and I came to Banaras instead, to study Hindi. The year was 1968.

'I found that admissions were closed in BHU. I went to another college, Mahatma Gandhi Kashi Vidyapeeth. There, the head of the Hindi department told me that even though there were seats, admissions had been closed. A lecturer who noticed my plight took me to the principal and presented my case. The principal took pity on me and issued an order for my admission. Before I proceed with the story, let me go back to my childhood because I want to tell you about Gowri Shankar.'

'Who is Gowri Shankar?'

Gaya Singh opens his eyes: 'Gowri Shankar was my guide and what you call a bosom friend—right from the time I was a little boy. He was instrumental in my getting admitted to school. I was four at the time and he was six. He was already going to school and I would sometimes accompany him because there was an orchard near the school and we would eat fruits all day.

'One day Gowri Shankar asked the teacher to give me admission in the first standard. The teacher said that I first needed to go to a nursery school. Gowri Shankar replied, "Don't worry about that, I will teach him." Imagine a boy of six saying that to a teacher! The teacher agreed to admit me in the first standard, provided I was able to memorise and recite a certain verse. I was given time to prepare.'

Gaya Singh shuts his eyes again to recite it. It is about Ram breaking Shiva's bow.

'The lines fascinated me so much,' he says, 'that I began to look for their source as I grew up. So much so, that I did a PhD on Tulsidas's works just so that I could trace them. But I simply couldn't find that particular verse. Only much later did I figure that the lines had come from the Bhat. The Bhat were people who, in the olden days, went from home to home telling stories in verse form. That was their source of living.

'I ran into the same teacher one day, decades after I had left school. I told him triumphantly that I had finally figured the source of the verse. He gave me a mischievous smile.

'Now let's go back to my childhood again. So the teacher gave me those lines to recite and when I was able to do so, he wrote my name in the register of the school. I was admitted to the first standard. Gowri Shankar came home and told my mother to get me some decent clothes. That was a challenge for her. We weren't really poor, in the sense that we had a farm and there was always sufficient food. But cash was often a problem.

'I remember that once, when my fees had to be paid, there was no money at home. My mother went to the neighbourhood jeweller to sell a piece of her jewellery. The jeweller scolded her, saying, "Your child is like my child." He loaned her the money.'

Gaya Singh's eyes well up at the memory. It's painful to see tears trickling down the cheeks of a man whose laughter is capable of waking up an entire locality. Fortunately, the bell rings and lunch arrives, sparing me more awkward moments.

'How did you get into BHU?' I ask him as we eat.

'Here too, Gowri Shankar played a role. He was a bright student, a topper all his life. He was already in BHU when I came to study at Kashi Vidyapeeth. One day when I was visiting him at the hostel—he was at the Broacha Hostel—he asked me to stay back for lunch. He said lunch was going to be special that day because the hostel was celebrating its anniversary. In the evening there was a function to mark the occasion, so we attended that as well.

'At the event the chief guest made a speech'—Gaya Singh puts his plate on the table and stands up to reenact the event—'I was so impressed by him that I asked Gowri Shankar who the man was. Gowri Shankar said, "Don't you know him? He is Hazari Prasad Dwivedi, our rector."

'I was shocked. I asked him, "You mean *the* Hazari Prasad Dwivedi?" He said yes. That very moment I resolved that, come what may, I *had* to study in BHU. I mean, when a giant littérateur like Hazari Prasad Dwivedi was associated with BHU, how could I even think of studying elsewhere? But the problem was that admissions were closed, all the seats were filled. I had to find a way.'

'So how did you get in?'

Gaya Singh doesn't give me a direct answer, dragging me instead down another memory lane. He has been doing this all afternoon, rushing me from one lane to another, like a child eager to show me all his toys at once. He not only keeps going back and forth in time but also breaks his story into branches and expects me to climb them, whereas I want to hold on to the trunk.

We finish lunch. A couple of hours later, I order tea and pakoras. But I still have no idea how he got admission in BHU, even though Gaya Singh has been talking animatedly all along. I, however, get an idea how he came to be portrayed the way he has been in *Kashi ka Assi*.

Close to six in the evening, Gaya Singh insists that I take a boat ride with him, right up to Rajghat and back to Assi, where he would treat me to dinner. I gladly agree: I need some fresh air.

From the boat, Banaras at this hour looks more like the handiwork of a celebrated art director than of Shiva. The entire riverfront could pass for the venue of a fairytale wedding. Each ghat is lit up in shades of red and blue and green, the darkness and the colours together airbrushing every visible sign of ugliness and decay. Banaras wasn't like this before.

Gaya Singh looks pleased at my amazement. I can sense he wants to talk, but conversation is impossible because of the noise of the motor. This is the longest I've seen him silent, and we still have a long way to go. The boat is approaching the illuminated bridge at Rajghat and will soon turn around and cover the seven kilometres to Assi.

By now I know how Gaya Singh got into BHU. He had resumed telling me his story as we walked from the hotel to Dashashwamedha to take the boat and I was finally able to gather how he pulled it off. It's a simple story. He had approached the students' union—led by an influential communist leader—which pressured the college administration into increasing the number of seats so that Gaya Singh could be accommodated.

On reaching Assi we walk past his house—it's a large house—and walk into the same restaurant where we had had dinner with Kashinath Singh the other night. He asks me to choose from the menu.

'So you joined Harishchandra College as soon as you finished your PhD?' I ask him.

'That's right. I joined as a lecturer in 1974 and retired as the principal in 2004. I was the vice-principal for a long time, and when the post of principal was offered to me I did not refuse because I did not want to be seen as an escapist from responsibilities.

'On becoming the principal, I changed the whole system. You see, many organisations, such as banks or other government bodies, hold their examinations in colleges. They not only use the college premises but also utilise the services of the college staff. For this, they pay a fee. Until I took over, the principal would be pocketing this fee—it is a huge sum.

'But I decided to distribute that money among the college staff who reported for duty during such exams. A teacher who used to get merely 500 rupees to invigilate began getting 4,000 rupees. Peons who got just 100 rupees for their services began getting 1,000 rupees. My successors must be cursing me today, but I earned the goodwill of a lot of people.'

I want to ask him whether he had tried joining BHU as a lecturer before finding a job in Harishchandra College but I decide to let it be. Common sense suggests that a BHU student wanting to be a teacher would first try his luck in BHU, so it is quite probable that he had applied but not succeeded. I am, however, in no mood to be sucked into another circuitous story. Instead, I ask him a question that's less likely to make him go in circles; it's a question I really want him to answer: why is he an atheist?

'What is God?' asks Gaya Singh. 'A man picks up a stone and chisels it, a Brahmin then chants some mantras and consecrates it, and the stone becomes god. How can I believe in such a god? Man is bigger than God, and God exists in all humans.

'As Hazari Prasad Dwivedi once said: Don't mix with people who kill the god inside you, mix with people who bring alive the god in you. I see god in everyone. That is why I easily mingle with people. If I sit with politicians, you will think I am one of them. If I sit with literary figures, you will think I am one of them.

'All kinds of people respect Dr Gaya Singh today, such is my stature. Even Kashinath Singh, who was not kind to me in *Kashi ka Assi*, had to admit this in the book: that while the other candidates who got rejected for lecturers' jobs in BHU were rejected because of their stupidity, Dr Gaya Singh got rejected because of his scholarship. He is so right. When the interviewer would ask me a question, I would ask him a counter-question. Obviously he was not going to give me the job.'

After dinner, I take an autorickshaw back to the hotel, where I feel the absence of Dr Gaya Singh. I have spent the entire day with him. I have heard him laugh. I have seen his tears. I have listened to his dramatic statements—about himself. It will take me a while to get used to the silence.

One question nags me, though, but I am not going to go back to Kashinath Singh for an answer: why did he choose to retain Dr Gaya Singh's name even though he changed the names of all the other characters in *Kashi ka Assi*?

42.

ASSI IS A Banaras within Banaras—more Banaras than the rest of Banaras.

When I first set foot in the neighbourhood three years ago, I had regarded it with awe. I had felt like a small boat lost in the ocean, no idea where the nearest land was. Today, after countless visits and spending considerable time with the author and a principal character of *Kashi ka Assi*, I feel I am finally ashore.

Yet, I find no depletion in my fascination for it. I can build an additional home here. Assi has everything. It has a spacious ghat as ancient as the Dashashwamedha. It has its share of temples. It has an open-air theatre. It has bookshops and boutiques. It has cafés and restaurants. Now it has a Zumba studio too. Assi is antique and chic at once.

And yet every morning and evening, it acquires the air of a village marketplace, as vendors take over the pavements, heaps of fresh vegetables attracting not only passersby but also cows. Washed clothes are heaped on the tables of launderers who are busy ironing them. Roadside eateries and tea stalls buzz with people. Cusswords and wisdom fly in the air. Atheists brush shoulders with the devout, each respectful of the other.

It's a pleasant winter morning. How I wish I can stay on for a few more days, but work beckons. If I want to keep returning to Banaras, I must keep my job. I have hot kachoris from a crowded stall run by a friendly man called Raja, and cross the road to Pappu's teashop.

The shop was started by Pappu's grandfather some eighty years ago. These days, due to old age and arthritis, Pappu hardly comes to the shop, which is now run by his son Manoj. I have passed the shop many times before and even thought of stopping to have tea, but the unsmiling Manoj would be too busy rinsing glass tumblers in hot water to acknowledge my presence, and I would move on.

This morning I realise that's the way he is. His shop, after all, is an institution, and by merely standing on its threshold you declare you are here to have tea. No invitation required, no acknowledgment necessary. So, for the first time, I am sipping Pappu's tea, handed to me by his son Manoj.

Carrying the tea, I step into the seating area, complete with tables and benches—and instantly step back. The room is packed with elderly men who seem to be considering a serious matter, and I feel like an intruder. I settle on a bench outside, under the now watchful gaze of Manoj.

The tea, for all its reputation, tastes pretty ordinary. Perhaps Manoj is able to read my mind. 'I will make you a special tea,' he tells me. I feel gratified by the gesture, since it comes from a man who doesn't usually acknowledge your presence.

He prepares black tea and to it adds spices, lemon juice and grated ginger. Just the kind of thing you would like on a chilly morning.

'Do you remember Kashinath Singh coming here?' I ask him.

'The tea I just gave you—that was his favourite.'

'Do the characters from *Kashi ka Assi* still come here?'

'Most of them are dead. Other than Gaya Singh, almost all of them have passed on.'

43.

THERE ARE—NOT surprisingly—many things Vishwanath in Banaras. There is a Vishwanath Jewellers, there is a Vishwanath Card Shop, there is a Vishwanath Hotel—one can go on.

Located in Vishwanath Gali, barely fifty steps from the Vishwanath Temple, is a small shop called Vishwanath Chaat Bhandar. It is run by a man called Raju Gupta, who can barely read or write and doesn't even know his age—he thinks he must be around thirty-two—but he adds spice to the life of Banarasis every evening.

I have been recommended this shop several times before by friends who regularly visit Banaras, it's just that I always spared myself the trouble of locating it. Walking up or down Vishwanath Gali itself is a challenge—you are forever stepping aside to make way for people who, unlike you, are not ambling around—and to spot a particular shop in it poses even more challenges.

But since I am leaving tomorrow and have time to kill, I decide to look for it. The shop turns out to be just a five-minute walk from my hotel, and now I am standing at it with a paper bowl in my hand. Raju serves me six pani-puris, one after the other. As the final act, he squeezes the juice of an entire lemon on the bowl, sprinkles spices and tops it up with a ladle-full of tamarind water. Drinking the mixture brings about instant satisfaction.

Reputations are rarely built through publicity but always through word of mouth. Raju's shop is an example of that. It's hidden in the gali, but people still find it. I try to make conversation with him but that proves impossible: there is a constant stream of impatient customers demanding to be served. He suggests he come over to my hotel once he shuts shop.

At ten o'clock the bell rings. I find Raju standing at the door. It takes me a few moments to recognise him because he has changed into a more presentable set of clothes. He has brought me a small box of sweets and a bundle of sweet paan.

'I learnt how to make pani-puris as a child,' he tells me. 'I learnt it from my father who ran a stall—he still runs it—in Allahabad. I have studied only up to Class 5. Very early on in life I realised that it was pointless to study because education does not guarantee you a job, whereas if you pick up a skill, you can easily earn 300 to 400 rupees a day.'

'How did you land up in Banaras?'

'I have an elder brother—elder to me by two or three years I think—who used to live with my grandfather in our village, very close to Allahabad. He was very naughty, always getting into some trouble or the other, so my father had decided to place him in the care of my grandfather.

'My grandfather was a very strict man. He was a chaprasi in the village school. One day, my brother stole 500 rupees from him and slipped away with his friends to Allahabad where they blew up the money on food and drink. When he got back home at night, my uncle was waiting for him with a stick. He began beating up my brother mercilessly.

'My grandfather intervened. He told my uncle, "He has stolen my money not yours, let me deal with him." My grandfather then decided to send my brother to a relative living in Banaras.

'My brother endured a lot of beatings and hardship at the relative's house. He did odd jobs for a while before deciding to sell pani-puri. He would walk on the road with a portable stand. Some days he would find a few customers, some days none. He did this for a few years before he decided to station himself at Vishwanath Gali—at the very spot where our shop stands today.

'He was lucky that the shopkeepers allowed him to position himself there. Normally they don't allow an outsider to conduct business in their gali. That way Banaras has been very kind to us.

'When I was in Class 5, I decided not to study further and came to Banaras to live with my brother. For many years I sold papad, walking on the roads, carrying a basket on my head. Then I got myself a cart and went around selling pani-puri. Together, my brother and I began to make a decent income.

'Then one day—this was about fifteen years ago—we decided to rent the shop outside which my brother would position himself every evening to sell pani-puri. We were required to pay 1.75 lakh rupees as security deposit apart from a monthly rent of 700 rupees. We borrowed 50,000 from a money-lender and the rest we managed with the help of relatives.

'By the grace of Baba Vishwanath, the shop began to do well. Baba has been very kind to us. As our reputation grew, people began calling us to weddings and other functions to set up stall. We are even called from faraway places like Bangalore and Chennai.

'Today, such events are our main source of income. And a few years ago, my brother got the contract to run the canteen at a medical college near Banaras. Money is no longer a problem. Until about fifteen years ago, I would be walking on the road all day to earn a meal, now I rarely have the time or the desire to eat.

'By the grace of Baba Vishwanath we now have three houses, not very far from the shop. The thing is, when I visit Baba, I never ask anything for myself. I always ask for the family. And he has always listened to me.

'Life was very difficult in rented houses. The landlords were very unkind to my children. They would make them do odd jobs, like fetching water for their bathrooms. I would lose my cool but my son would say, "Papa, I am the one fetching the water, why are you getting worked up?"

'One day I went to Baba and asked him to give us two or three houses so that we never have to stay in a rented house again. Sure enough, he gave us three houses. We were able to get loans from banks and overnight, we came to own three houses. This was about two years ago.'

'How often do you visit Baba?'

'As often as I can. Almost daily.'

'But there is always a long queue.'

'I can't afford to stand in a queue, sir. There is so much work to be done. I just walk in. Most people at the temple know me by now. Even the policemen on duty are my regular customers. They let me in. Then there are days when, in spite of wanting to visit the temple, I am unable to. On such days, Baba himself comes to me.'

'How?'

'He visits me in my dreams. He always comes in the form of a snake. It playfully chases me, coils itself around me, pretends to bite me.'

'How old are your children?'

'My daughter is thirteen and my son nine. Now my sole purpose in life is to educate them so that they get good jobs. I am praying to Baba for that. I am willing to make any number of sacrifices, but I want to see them settled with decent jobs, maybe as officers in a bank.

'There is something else I am praying to Baba for. I want him to find me a shop on the main road. As you must be aware, demolition is going on around the temple for the building of a corridor. The oldest parts, which had some of the best-known shops of Banaras, are already gone. From what I gather, they will soon demolish the buildings on Vishwanath Gali as well. If that happens, my shop will also go.'

'Wouldn't it make more sense to pray that the demolition stops?'

'No sir. The demolition, as I see it, has been willed by Baba himself. Even a leaf can't move in Banaras without Baba's consent, so how can one carry out such large-scale demolition if Baba doesn't want it that way? Baba wants the encroachments around his temple to go. People carrying out the project—like [Narendra] Modi—are merely his tools.'

44.

I RETURN AFTER two months to find the ghats of Banaras crowded with penises hanging from ash-coated torsos.

It's indeed a man's world—even the world inhabited by those who have discarded attachments, desires and also their clothes—because one simply can't even imagine the existence of female equivalents of Naga sadhus, leave alone the sight of such women crowding into public places. Female sadhus, if anything, don extra layers of clothing.

Conquest of desire can be truly put to the test only if both men and women go about naked without sexual thoughts pervading their minds, but why take chances? Also, think of the stampede likely to be caused by onlookers who are under no obligation to not watch nor lust.

But I find even the naked male sadhus getting attention. They have pitched tents in Banaras after having purified themselves at Allahabad—where the kumbh mela is still on—and are playing Shiva to pilgrims stopping by for their blessings. Banaras is choking with pilgrims: Shivaratri is around the corner and they are arriving in hordes. Many of them are coming—like the sadhus—straight from Allahabad.

Aimless in Banaras

This morning, the queue leading to the Vishwanath Temple has stretched right up to Dashashwamedha. By the time the man at the end of it got to the sanctum sanctorum, a London-bound flight from Delhi would have reached its destination. At the police booth in Godowlia, a man imitating Ameen Sayani is tirelessly speaking into the microphone, helping to unite families that have got separated: 'Pyare Lal from Deoria, wherever you are, please come to the booth right away, your wife is inconsolable.' One can only hope that Pyare Lal has heard the announcement and soon rejoins his wife.

The long queue, the milling crowds, the incessant announcements—all this is making me dizzy. When I had returned to Banaras after three years, I felt as if I had never left, but now when I am back after barely two months, I feel displaced. To reclaim my familiarity I walk to Darbhanga Ghat, and as I walk a question nags me: Is God more likely to listen to you if you stand in a queue for hours on an auspicious day for just a fraction-of-a-second glimpse of him than if you walk into a deserted wayside temple for a prolonged one-on-one audience with him on any slow day of the year?

At Darbhanga Ghat I sit on the steps after having ordered some tea from a stall. A man passing by smiles at me, as if we've met before, and when I smile back he walks over to sit next to me.

'Where are you from?' he asks.

'Calcutta. And you?'

'I am from Bikaner. Is Calcutta a good place to do business?'

'I am sure it is. There are a whole lot of people from Rajasthan doing business in Calcutta.'

'Oh really? What can I sell there?'

'Anything under the sun.'

'Tell me, *yeh behenchod yahaan nange kyon ghoom rahe hain?*'—Why are these sister-fuckers roaming around naked?

'That's how Naga sadhus are.'

'Do they have no consideration for the mothers and sisters who are here?'

Just then I hear an outburst. The assistant of a naked sadhu has spotted an Indian woman trying to take a picture of his boss on the sly. 'He is not one of those sadhus who like to pose!' he thunders. 'He can reduce you to ashes with his gaze!'

The boss remains unperturbed, his face as expressionless as his dick.

45.

MY EYES QUICKLY get used to the sight of dicks and bare bums as I walk from Darbhanga Ghat in the direction of Assi. I spot a naked sadhu who is standing outside his tent and speaking on the phone. His demeanour is that of a CEO who has stepped out of a meeting to answer an important call.

I come across another sadhu, who is also speaking on the phone. His dick is out in the open but his eyes are protected by fluorescent sunglasses. With clothes, he would have passed off for a menacing gangster, not that he looks any less menacing without them.

It isn't such a bad idea, becoming a sadhu. You can strut around naked, pretending to have given it all up and yet retain your mobile phone; you can get food without having to work for it; you can attract devotees by virtue of your mere appearance; you can pitch tent in a scenic location and enjoy its charms free of cost. The palace at Darbhanga Ghat is today a hotel where a night costs a fortune, but the feel of the Ganga you get from a sadhu's tent is priceless.

I happen to enter one such tent after my eyes meet those of its occupant, a young, cheerful sadhu who is not naked at the moment and has a loincloth covering his genitals. He gestures to me to sit next to him. He already has a visitor—a Frenchman—who is bitterly complaining about another Naga sadhu he has just met: 'He is always barking like a dog. No positive energy.'

When tea is served to us in plastic cups, the Frenchman says: 'Hope no Ganga water in this. Ganga water in Rishikesh, no problem. Ganga water in Varanasi, little problem.' The Frenchman's English is as good or bad as the sadhu's, but they are conversing like two friends catching up after a long gap.

Once the Frenchman leaves, the sadhu turns to me. Suddenly, I am overcome by the same feeling: as if we are two friends catching up after a period. As our conversation meanders from one subject to another, I am offered plenty of food for thought: 'You can buy food but you cannot buy appetite'; 'you can buy a bed but you cannot buy sleep'; 'you can buy pleasures but you cannot buy happiness'.

Not to be outdone, I too offer him some nuggets of wisdom: 'Nothing is permanent, everything is transient'; 'God is inside you, it is foolish to look for him elsewhere'; 'people are born to die, once we accept this fact of life we won't need God'. Roaming the streets of Banaras, I realise, can sufficiently equip you to engage in a dialogue with a sadhu who is supposed to know more than you.

The sadhu appears pleased with my company. 'Ever since I came to Banaras,' he says, 'I've been looking to make a disciple. I have finally found a suitable candidate. Get a sacred thread tomorrow, I shall initiate you.'

'Why did you become a sadhu?'

'I didn't want to stay home because of my father. Such a cruel man, that mother-fucker! He behaved as if he did me a great favour by producing me. Did I plead with him to bring me into this world? He chose to sleep with my mother and that's how I was born—he didn't do me any favour. Then why did he expect me to always act according to his wishes?'

'But aren't most parents like that?'

'He was a brutal bastard. He would beat me savagely if I scored less marks than the boy living next door. I had no desire to live in such a family, in such a society. One day I decided enough was enough.'

'But why a sadhu?'

'As I told you, I didn't want to belong to a society where marks matter, where parents beat you up brutally just because you have scored low marks.'

'Why do you people go around naked?'

'Everybody is naked under their clothes. Why pretend to be not naked by merely putting on some bits of cloth? The real clothes are respect, compassion, conduct. If you earn no respect, if you don't have compassion in your heart, if your conduct is bad, do you think clothes can conceal those shortcomings?'

'Do sadhus have sex?'

'Let's not go there,' he laughs.

'I am curious. Do you still have desire or do you consider all women to be your mothers and sisters?'

'I am not seeking mothers and sisters,' he laughs louder. 'If that was the case I might as well have stayed with the mother and sister I left behind at home.'

'Since you have severed all connections, why do you need a smartphone?'

'To stay informed—we need to know what's going on in the world—and also to stay in touch with fellow sadhus from our sect. The phone makes it easier to coordinate our movements. We get to know where to reach on which day and at what time.'

The sadhu then gets up and, reminding me to get a sacred thread the next morning, walks down the steps of the ghat. He unwinds his hair from his topknot, removes his loincloth and gets into the water. I resume my walk in the direction of Assi, wondering if I should indeed return to him with a sacred thread. I realise it may not be necessary because, during the short time I spent with him, we became friends on Facebook—and that should suffice.

46.

AT ASSI GHAT I breathe easy. It feels like getting off a crowded bus at a familiar destination.

I survey the river. The migratory birds are gone but there are far too many noisy motorised boats. The tourist season is still at its peak. This time I see more foreigners on the ghats than I ever have—not wide-eyed first-timers but the kind wearing kurtas and rudraksha beads. They just might have a better understanding of Banaras than I do, meticulous as they are in researching a place before setting foot in it.

This evening another Westerner will arrive in Banaras, my American friend Jerome Armstrong, who has just written a book titled *Calcutta Yoga* and is working on another one, a journey along the Ganga from Bengal to its source in the Himalayas. So far our meetings have taken place in Calcutta and Chennai but never in Banaras, even though he has been here several times before. He is, at the moment, in Allahabad.

Assi Ghat bears a deserted look as usual. I am sure it has got its share of visitors at this hour, but it's just that the Dashashwamedha is so crowded that Assi always appears empty in comparison. I wonder why pilgrims are so blinkered as to stick to Dashashwamedha and rarely ever venture to Assi. They have their reasons, I am sure. One reason I can think of—though I could be wrong—is that the lay pilgrim is usually a poor man who comes to Banaras bearing the twin burdens of poverty and religious obligation. Once he is done with the rituals at Dashashwamedha, he wants to head home. Banaras, for him, is a pillar of faith and not a destination—and the pillar's circumference rarely ever exceeds the span of Dashashwamedha. And since sadhus invariably remain close to pilgrims, they too are hardly ever seen at Assi.

But right now I do spot an old sadhu here. All this while he was asleep under a tree and is now sitting up. His silhouette looks familiar. I walk up to him. He looks shabby and very ill.

'Aren't you Amrit Das Phawrawala?' I ask him.

He nods feebly.

'I met you three years ago. I don't think you will remember me, but I remember everything about you. Your grandfather was a Marwari who had married a French woman in Pondicherry. You went to medical school but dropped out to become a sadhu.'

He smiles at me. The smile is laboured. I find that some of his teeth are now missing. I met him only three years ago but he looks withered by ten. I want to ask him what he has been up to all this while, but it is evident that time has not been kind to him.

'Take care,' I tell him. Someday, sooner than later, he will be found lifeless, perhaps under a tree. It could be this very tree. His death won't matter to anyone. To the people who might have shed a tear or two, he is already long dead.

I stand on the steps leading to the Dashashwamedha, watching the crowds disperse after the Ganga Aarti. I hear someone call out my name. It's Jerome, my friend. We were trying to locate each other throughout the duration of the aarti but in vain. The place was so packed—the large number of Westerners and sadhus adding to the attendance—that trying to spot a familiar face seemed no less challenging than finding a needle in a haystack.

Now that the crowd has almost melted away, it is not only easy to spot someone but also hear if your name is called. It's not just the pilgrims who are blinkered, even Indian tourists are. For most of them, Banaras is today synonymous with the Ganga Aarti. They arrive shortly before the aarti begins and leave as soon as it is over. Look and leave—one more item on the bucket-list ticked. No one stays on to experience Dashashwamedha minus its pilgrims. That's a luxury Banarasis like to indulge in— sometimes, they find company in outsiders like Jerome and me.

In my experience, the true flavour of a place reveals itself only after the crowd is gone; but if that realisation dawns on every single person in the crowd, then a place would be crowded at all times.

Locals are now occupying the cots on which the young men performing the aarti had stood. The badminton court is being set up. An idli-seller has materialised in the space that was jam-packed until minutes ago. His idlis are hot. The river is black; the riverside street lamps emphasising the long curve that's Banaras. We are standing at the centre of the curve.

'How was Allahabad?' I ask Jerome.

'Oh man, don't even ask. I'm sore.'

During the one day he spent at Allahabad to experience the kumbh, he walked 30,000 steps—his phone told him so—and spent the night on a boat, waking with eighty mosquito bites on his arms and forehead. To get to Banaras, he stood in a packed train for four hours. And now he desperately needs to catch up on sleep. We part ways, deciding to meet at the same spot the next morning to watch the sunrise.

Once he leaves I buy myself hot idlis. As I eat, I am reminded of what the manager of the lodge where I stayed in 2015 had told me: 'South Indian food in Banaras tastes any day better than the food you get in south India.' I now find myself nodding in agreement.

47.

VERY FEW THINGS in the world happen with the same precision as the sunrise. Yet no two sunrises are the same. The weather, the location, whether you are alone or have company, if you have company then what kind of company, your state of mind—these are some of the factors that decide the quality of a sunrise.

This morning's sunrise makes Dashashwamedha look uglier than ever. There are far too many people, and to cater to them, far too many boatmen and priests. Sunrise, in my head, is something that sets off human activity at a lazy pace, but right now it only serves in illuminating—and thus amplifying—an ongoing frenzy.

There is a new—and grotesque—addition to the ghat: a rubber quay, a patchwork of yellow and blue, projecting into the river. The idea, evidently, is to accommodate more boats and I am sure many would see this new installation as 'development of Banaras'.

Jerome regards the scene with amusement. He has slept well and appears more receptive to what's going on around him. We decide to take a boat ride to Assi. From the cacophony of the ghat, we plunge into the noise of motorised boats. The painted bodies of the boats, which once upon a time displayed names of banks and charitable institutions, now advertise travel portals and apps. A motorboat crossing us right now is spreading awareness about the HopOnIndia audio guide app. Our boat, though, is a country boat.

'Should I hook my boat to that boat?' the young boatman points to the passing motorboat. This is the first time I've come across such a suggestion and it irritates me.

'We are not in a hurry,' I tell him.

The motorboat whizzes past, carrying a group of white-skinned tourists wearing fixed smiles. I wish I could read their minds.

I've done this route—Dashashwamedha to Assi, or the reverse—more times than I can count, but each time the riverfront looks new from the boat, as if it's my first time in Banaras.

As we cross Manasarovar Ghat, I find a man doing the dund, better known as 'Hindu pushups', which call for far greater muscular strength than the regular ones. On another ghat upstream, an elderly man in a maroon loincloth is swinging a mace. Nearly every ghat has its share of bathers, the bright saris of the women looking even brighter under the ascending sun.

'How deep is the river here?' I ask the boatman.

'Very deep,' he replies, 'easily seventy to eighty feet.'

He could be right. A river sustaining an entire civilisation has to be that deep. I have never come across a human swimming across its entire breadth, at least in Banaras, though I have seen buffaloes venturing quite far midstream.

Come to think of it, I was born in a city by the Ganga, lived quite close to its banks until the age of twenty-three and later cremated my mother under its gaze, and yet I know so little about the river. Jerome, on the other hand, has even been to its source—trekking up the final few kilometres without another human in sight—and actually put icicles into his mouth. I've only been as far up as Rishikesh, and visited very few settlements located by the river. Yet I feel a sense of entitlement when it comes to the Ganga. Entitlement is only a notion, experience is real. I have a long way to go.

After whiling away some time at Assi, we decide to walk to Jerome's hotel. He has got me some leather sleeves for my fountain pens. He had shown me the hotel from the boat. It sits at a height at Manasarovar Ghat and overlooks the river.

As we walk, we are waylaid by an off-duty doam at Harishchandra Ghat. 'Hello, gentleman,' he greets Jerome while ignoring me. 'How are you?'

'I am good,' Jerome replies.

'Which country you coming from?'

'From America.'

'America? Oh, very good, very good. Come with me.'

He leads us to the platform of a shut temple overlooking the burning ghat. He dusts the floor with a gamchha and motions us to sit. His name is Madroo Chaudhari. He is sixty-five years old and has been cremating bodies ever since he was a child.

'In Banaras, there are two burning ghats, Manikarnika and Harishchandra,' he says in English. 'Both very famous. Here, when bodies burn, no smell. Do you get smell? No smell!'

I find Jerome agreeing. He says he had recently been to a cremation ground in Delhi and there the stench had been unbearable.

'Why don't people use the electric crematorium?' Jerome asks him.

'Here there is electric crematorium, see the chimney? But not many people using it. Electric crematorium like a jail. Body go inside iron gate, like criminal going to jail. But when using wood, you watch end of life, in just three hours.'

At the moment two pyres are burning at the ghat and, from time to time, specs of ash fly into our faces. When a spec lands on my eyelid, Madroo Chaudhari dusts it off with the same gamchha.

'See there, another body,' he points to a boat that is moving from the ghat towards the middle of the river. It is carrying a shrouded corpse that is soon offloaded into the water. 'Fish will eat it now,' the doam says.

He tells us about the unclaimed bodies that are brought for cremation; he says their cremation is usually paid for by the doam with the help of donations. It would be, therefore, very kind of Jerome if he made a small donation. He has finally come to the point. Jerome parts with a crisp 500-rupee note.

'Are your children also in the cremation business?' I ask him.

'No, they are not,' he replies, switching over to Hindi, 'they are not illiterate like me, they went to college. I have seen difficult days. Our caste was looked down upon. Now there is not so much discrimination. People are slowly realising that the colour of blood, no matter whose blood it is, is red.'

48.

THAT BANARAS IS not beautiful but extremely photogenic is a fact that dawned on me long ago. Now it is reiterating itself at every step that I walk from Jerome's hotel back to Dashashwamedha and my own hotel. Each Naga sadhu camped on the ghats makes for a good portrait. The milling tourists also make a good subject: they stick out like white boats on a green river. Tourists clicking sadhus also make for good photographs: curiosity face-to-face with belief, the modern encountering the ancient. And when you zoom out on your subjects to include the red sandstone structures on one side and the river on the other, your camera puts Banaras in perspective. And yet so much of Banaras gets left out.

It is impossible to capture the city in its entirety in a single frame. That could be true for many other cities as well, but more so for Banaras because here you cannot claim entirety. Attempt to use the word 'entire' in your description of Banaras and the inevitable wise guy in your audience will nudge you: 'No, you have left such-and-such thing out.'

Now, suddenly, I find two young men wearing skull caps walking ahead of me. I follow them, eager to know where they are headed, but I lose them in the crowds at Dashashwamedha. Before they can totally disappear, I manage to get the skull caps in the frame—two white dots in the sea of colours, dominated by saffron—and realise that the pictures I have been clicking so far were incomplete.

Back in the hotel I go through all the pictures I've just taken. One picture grabs my attention. It was taken somewhere near Prabhu Ghat and has many things in the frame: boatmen hanging around waiting for custom, tourists walking past, a boy looking for buyers for his flutes. The central figure is a saffron-robed sadhu seated in the lotus pose, his shoes neatly placed next to him. He is facing the green river, which has several tourist-laden boats.

I zoom out the image a bit and crop it. It now shows only the meditating sadhu, his shoes, the river, and precisely two boats. The noise of Banaras is cut out and there is only calm. A new realisation dawns: framing the camera is akin to framing the mind. Even in a crowd, you can be alone, and even in noise, there can be calm.

49.

'WE CAN TELL if someone is on the verge of death,' Kali Kant Dubey tells me. 'The pulse becomes weak and the limbs begin to swell.'

Dubey is a caretaker at Mukti Bhawan, where people come to stay when they hear death knocking at their door. Since no one—neither Dubey, nor doctors—can predict the precise hour of death, one is allowed to stay for a fortnight. If they don't die but still look like they are going to, any moment, they are given four more days. If they still don't breathe their last, they are sent home.

The 1908-built Mukti Bhawan, stately enough to pass as the bungalow of a minister, is tucked away from a crowded road, barely a few minutes' walk from Godowlia. The lane leading to it is milling with young women in skinny-fit jeans, their cackle a contrast to the silence of death prevailing in the corridors of the building.

I wonder how those about to die look at those who have just begun their journey in life. With envy? Indifference? Bitterness? Resignation? Acceptance? I suspect most of those dying don't like to believe they are dying—they always hope to buy some more time either from God or doctors—and it calls for either immense courage or utmost hopelessness to recognise that the end is near.

Dubey tells me, 'We don't admit people below the age of sixty. They must look like they are dying. We charge twenty rupees a day. They must be accompanied by at least four members of their family. Four, because the moment they die the body needs to be moved out. As long as the body is inside, we cannot continue with our daily rituals like aarti and bhajan.

'We have Mangala aarti at four in the morning. The singing of bhajans starts at six and goes on till eight. In the evening, too, there is singing of bhajans from five to six, and aarti at night from nine to ten.

'The inmates are administered Ganga water thrice a day, at ten in the morning, at noon, and at three in the afternoon. All kinds of people come here, the rich as well as the poor. Only recently we had the dying relatives of an MLA and a police commissioner staying with us. On an average I see nine to ten people dying here every month.

'There are 84 lakh spirits in the air waiting to be reborn, either as humans, dogs, birds, insects, and so on. But if you die in Kashi, you are set free from the cycle of rebirths.'

'Can I take a look inside?' I ask him.

'By all means,' he says. 'At the moment we have only one elderly woman staying with us.'

The building, like most old-fashioned buildings, is constructed around a courtyard. Ten of its rooms are available to the dying. It was built by the Dalmia family, though I am not sure—neither is Dubey, who is only thirty-five—whether it always served as a home for the dying. It is quite likely that these rooms once served as bedrooms.

Around a tap in the courtyard, four men—relatives of the inmate—are brushing their teeth. The door of the inmate's room is slightly ajar and I see only darkness inside.

'When was the last time someone died here?' I ask Dubey.

'The day before yesterday.'

'You watch people breathing their last. Has that taught you something about life?'

'Yes. Whoever is born has to die.'

50.

THERE WAS—OR is—an age-defiant man called Babaji, living somewhere in the Himalayas, never sighted by anyone except a few deserving disciples, one of them being Shyama Charan Lahiri.

Lahiri, who lived from 1828 to 1895, established a reputation as a spiritual guru even though he remained a householder all his life. He was essentially a Banarasi, even though his work—he was employed in British days as a bookkeeper—took him to other places. He was posted in Ranikhet when he encountered Babaji and was initiated into Kriya Yoga, a forgotten yogic practice that awakened spiritual powers while arresting decay of tissues in the body.

The technique descended from Lahiri to his own worthy disciples, one of them being a man called Yukteshwar, who, in turn, passed it on to his own followers, including Mukunda Lal Ghosh, better known to the world as Paramhansa Yogananda.

Yogananda travelled to the West and spread awareness about Kriya Yoga and its lineage. He acquired celebrity status, more so after authoring the bestseller, *Autobiography of a Yogi*. Among the Westerners impressed by him was the writer J.D. Salinger, who kept a picture of Shyama Charan Lahiri in his study—or was it the bedroom.

Yogananda died rather young, of heart failure, in 1952, barely three months after his fifty-ninth birthday, in California. By then, in Calcutta, his younger brother Bishnu Charan Ghosh had made a name for himself as a body-builder and a yoga guru. He founded the Ghosh Yoga College, and one of his pupils, Bikram Choudhury, went on to earn worldwide reputation as a yoga teacher before he—quite recently—fled from America because he found himself slapped with charges of rape.

It's a fascinating chain—right from the venerable Babaji to the disgraced Bikram—with several vital links in between with their own stories. My friend Jerome's book *Calcutta Yoga*—no, it's not a handbook on yoga—disentangles that chain and tells the stories of the many people separated by time and geography but united by lineage.

The link that belongs to Banaras is Shyama Charan Lahiri. Jerome and I are now standing in a house-turned-ashram called Satyalok, an oasis of silence located in the bustle of a gali off Chowsatti Ghat. Here the ashes of Lahiri lie buried. There is also a shrine of Babaji. Like Shiva, he too has been physically depicted: a wiry man seated in the lotus pose, locked palms placed on the lap. His statue looks very life-like, as if he is keenly watching us.

Not very far from this place, located in another gali, is the house where Lahiri spent the later part of his life. The wooden door leading to it is now shut. A nameplate on the door says 'B. Lahiry, 31/58, Madanpura, Varanasi'—the name obviously belonging to one of his descendants. According to the owner of a shop that faces the house, it opens only once a year, on Guru Purnima, for devotees.

I must confess that once upon a time, not very long ago, I was enamoured of *Autobiography of a Yogi* and the characters described in it, especially Lahiri himself. Not anymore. After having cremated at Manikarnika the woman who helped me take my first steps, I don't find the need to walk holding the fingers of a guru. The ghats and galis of Banaras—where time and again you are reminded of the biggest and unshakeable truth of life, that anyone born has to die—teach you to be your own guru.

Outside the shop facing Lahiri's house is a wooden bench, seated on which is a large Swiss man. At first I think he is a tourist catching his breath. Then he tells us that he comes here every year—just to sit outside Lahiri's house and feel his presence.

Outside Lahiri's house—I don't know how—Jerome and I get separated. He was here a moment ago, when I was talking to the Swiss man, and now I don't see him. Maybe he was sniffing around for material and has strayed into another alley. It is easy for outsiders to get lost in the maze. I try his phone but can't reach him. Alone, I wander deeper into Madanpura—and make a big discovery.

51.

THESE DAYS MOST of the 'Banarasi silk' saris you get in Banaras are neither Banarasi nor silk. They are synthetic imitations that come from Surat, in Gujarat. And the ones that are still made in Banaras are mostly woven by machines. Therefore the genuine Banarasi sari, handmade locally, has become a rarity and costs a fortune.

This discovery, which I make as I venture deeper into Madanpura, makes me glad that I never thought of purchasing a sari in Banaras. I also discover—even though this discovery is not surprising—that the saris that Hindus flaunt at weddings are woven, more often than not, by Muslims.

Madanpura is a Muslim-dominated neighbourhood, a part of Banaras's ecosystem, peppered with workshops where fabric is woven, its alleys woven into the fabric that is Banaras. I follow the clatter of a loom into an aged building, where a lone man in a skull cap is at work. He switches off the machine so that we can talk. He is the second person I come across in Madanpura—I have just spent some time at a sari shop where the customers were all Hindus—who tells me that a lot of the stuff now sold in Banaras comes from Surat.

'You are a learned man,' the skull-capped weaver tells me, 'you must be aware how famous Banarasi silk saris used to be. But a few decades ago, some people began propagating the idea, nationally as well as internationally, that wearing silk amounted to himsa, violence.

'Silk, I am sure a learned person like you already knows, is made from the saliva of a worm. The worm dies once the silk is extricated. It takes twenty to twenty-five worms to generate one thread of silk. So these people began to say that it is unethical to wear something that is manufactured in a process that involves the killing of creatures. The thought began to catch on, and between the years 2000 and 2005, we saw a steep decline in the demand for silk.

'Silk, let me tell you, is the best fabric you can get in the entire world. There is no match for it. It is free of chemicals that harm the skin. But then, people fell for the anti-silk campaign. As the demand dropped, the vacuum began to be filled by saris from Surat made of synthetic silk. Weavers began to find other jobs. Until about twenty-five years ago, I too used to weave saris by hand. Now I use this loom, even though I haven't forgotten the art.

'Since labour is very cheap in Surat, the cost of the saris is also much less. A sari from Surat usually costs between 10,000 and 15,000 rupees. It can pass off as a pure Banarasi silk sari. A handmade Banarasi silk sari, with intricate zari work, will cost anywhere between 1 and 2 lakh rupees.

'These days, even much of the zari work is done on the computer. There are electronic jacquards that come from China, and you only need to feed the design into the computer. But a computer is not capable of the intricacies that can be achieved by the human hand, that is why hand-woven zaris cost a lot more.

'The Surat sari has other advantages. You can wear it any number of times before you wash it and you can wash it the way you like. A pure silk sari can only be dry-cleaned.'

'Where does the silk come from?'

'The silk for Banarasi saris has always come from China and Korea.'

'Why is it imported?'

'Their silk is far superior to what you get in India.'

'Then why are they called Banarasi saris, and not Chinese or Korean saris?'

'It doesn't matter where the silk is sourced from, what matters is the weave. If the weaving is done in Banaras, it has to be called a Banarasi sari. When you walked in, I was weaving a cotton dress material. The cotton has come from Coimbatore, but the fabric will be considered Banarasi. How stupid of me, we have been talking all this while and I haven't asked your name.'

I give my name and ask for his. He is Imtiaz Ahmed.

'Have you always lived in Banaras?' I ask him.

'My family has lived here for 200 years. My great-grandfather died in 1935 at the age of 120. My grandfather too lived to be 100 and he died in 1972. My father, however, died young, at the age of seventy.'

'I hope you live as long as your grandfather. How old are you now?'

'I am fifty-one. Once upon a time, Madanpura used to be populated by rich Bengalis (that explains its proximity to Bengali Tola), whereas Muslims used to live closer to the river. I am talking about the final years of the Mughal rule, the time of Bahadur Shah Zafar. Over the years, the rich Bengalis began to return to their native places and sold their properties to Muslims. Even this house, where we are standing now, was sold to my grandfather by the zamindar of a place called Kakina, in Bengal.

'So we are a part of Banaras's history, we are as Banarasi as our Hindu neighbours, and we live together peacefully. Each one is happy doing his own thing and no one interferes in the other's life. Occasionally, though, there are people who try to create trouble between the two communities.

'The trouble-makers are invariably outsiders. When such troubles erupt, the mischievous elements have a good time. Muslims walking through Hindu-dominated alleys—which they have to in order to supply garments to the wholesalers—often find their caps plucked with hooks by people from terraces.

'Fortunately, elders and intellectuals from both communities sit together and make people see sense. They explain to us that Hindus and Muslims depend on each other. Without orders from Hindu shops, Muslim weavers will starve, and without supplies from Muslim weavers, Hindu shopkeepers will starve.

'There are politicians who want to divide people on the basis of religion. They are asking Hindus to hate Muslims. Their ploy may work in other places but not in Banaras. Here we stand at Dashashwamedha and look at the river even while priests are conducting rituals—nobody questions our presence.

'My grandfather and father have spent countless nights lying on the sands by the river and returned home well after midnight. I too have done that during my younger days. Banaras is not like any other place. It is different. Hatred will never take seed here.'

52.

AFTER WATCHING ANOTHER sunrise together, Jerome and I are having breakfast at Bona Café. It's a low-seating, Korean-style restaurant located in one of the alleys of Bengali Tola, not very far from the home of Shyama Charan Lahiri and the workshop of the weaver.

Tomorrow both of us are leaving Banaras. He will proceed to Rishikesh, I will return to the grind in Calcutta.

I am tempted to tag along. I love Rishikesh and carry fond memories of it. Memories of a place like Rishikesh—where you never lose sight of the Ganga gurgling out from between two mountains—can hardly be unpleasant. Often referred to as the capital of yoga, its reputation today overshadows that of Haridwar. There was a time when tourists went to Haridwar and, depending on how much time they had, also visited Rishikesh. Now it's the other way round.

But Rishikesh, despite its charms, much of which is slowly declining due to the mushrooming of resorts and yoga schools, is, at best, an escape. You go there seeking respite, and once you realise you've had your break, you want to come back. Banaras, on the other hand, is a way of life. If you walk its ghats and galis without purpose you become a Banarasi in no time and want to linger on.

Being a Banarasi is the way to be if happiness is your aim. People in big cities, who are unable to find peace despite material comforts, often flock to swanky ashrams of self-proclaimed spiritual gurus in search of verbal—and sometimes herbal—balms. The rich want to get richer while the powerful want to cling to power, and to source the mental strength required for it they go to gurus, who know exactly which buttons to press. Seeing the rich and mighty bow before them, the lesser mortals too get inspired.

In Banaras, no one preaches to you. You learn from its pyres and its people. The pyres tell you that no matter who you are, you aren't ultimately worth more than a heap of ash. And its people show you that since you are anyway going to be a heap of ash someday, you might as well be happy. And the easiest way to be happy—as the retired peon I once met at the akhara taught me—is to be satisfied with whatever little comes your way.

This perhaps explains why I am overcome by sadness each time I leave Banaras. When I walk its ghats and galis, I find myself free of fears and insecurities because I am made to realise, time and again, that, in the end, nothing matters.

After finishing breakfast we order green tea. Bona Café is a nice place to linger in. It's right in the heart of Banaras but still not Banarasi. A monastic silence hangs between its walls, something appreciated by Westerners who like to read or work while they are eating. The alley on which it is located could well belong to Rishikesh: there are more people from the West there than locals. When we were walking to the café, I happened to overhear a foreigner asking a shopkeeper for '*khuhttey ke liye biskut*'—biscuits for dogs.

Jerome too likes to do his writing in this café. Unlike me, he takes notes and jots down thoughts on the phone. He tells me that today he is going to write about his previous night's experience at a temple. The priest, he says, was dancing on one leg and the fire burning inside the temple was so fierce that it became impossible for him to linger, but when he wanted to leave he had found the exit blocked by a bunch of people who said he could leave only after the ceremony was over.

'Really? Where's this temple?'

'Right at Mankarnika.'

'I must find out.'

I leave Jerome to himself and begin my walk in the direction of—well, I don't know. I walk through the galis, past sleeping dogs and around bulls blocking the path. I marvel at the number of guest houses and eateries with chic names that now lie hidden in the galis of Banaras, their locations all too well known to those who care to search the internet.

Banaras may be ancient, but it has also changed with times without losing its halo of ancientness, and that could be one of the reasons for its longevity. It is like that erudite, ageless grandfather who flaunts an exquisite collection of fountain pens but relies on the laptop and phone to stay in touch. Such men always make for interesting company.

There is, however, one thing that Banaras, for all its erudition, has not been able to tell me about itself. Maybe I haven't come across those who know the answer. In all references to the Vishwanath Temple in books and newspaper reports dating back to the nineteenth century, Shiva has been referred to by another of his many names: Vishweshwar. When exactly did the all-important switch to Vishwanath happen?

Not that the answer is going to make a great difference to my life. But yes, had the switch not happened, my countless namesakes and I might have been called differently.

53.

AFTER A NAP I stand outside my hotel and watch Godowlia warming up for the evening. I find the ache returning. Tomorrow this time I will be on the way to the airport, carrying Banaras in my head and in the pages of my notebook. My aimlessness—which has only sharpened the focus on my aims—will come to an end.

It is difficult to be aimless in the city where you are earning your living. A full-time job accords a pattern to your life as you divide time between home and office, and the pattern gets more constricting as your roles expand and responsibilities mount. One can still find time to be aimless, perhaps on a Sunday, but such aimlessness will only be contrived. Also, in order to be aimless, one must walk—Banaras forces you to walk, whereas bigger cities hardly give you the space.

A familiar face—a man wearing a cap and spectacles—is walking past me. But I am unable to place him. He isn't a long-lost acquaintance or friend but someone I've met very recently. Then it strikes me that he is the voice of Godowlia, the Ameen Sayani of Banaras, who sits at the police booth almost throughout the day, helping families that have got separated and generally keeping passersby entertained. I've got so accustomed to the sight of him making incessant announcements that I feel I know him well.

During an auspicious period such as this, when a sea of humanity descends on Godowlia, his voice serves as a landmark as important as geographical ones. I hurry behind him and introduce myself. His name is Kaushal Kishore Mishra, he is sixty-five years old, and he is walking back to the booth after a short break at home, which is barely a kilometre away.

It turns out that he was indeed a big fan of Ameen Sayani, and that made him join All-India Radio as a casual announcer way back in 1980. He would get 25 rupees per shift. By the time he left radio in 1992, the remuneration had gone up to 160 per shift. He didn't leave; his services were terminated.

In 1991, he found out that AIR had vacancies for full-time announcers. He applied but didn't get absorbed. He went to court and was sacked in 1992. The case dragged on till 2005, when his petition was dismissed. That same year, he began coming to the police booth at Godowlia.

'I continued the fight because it was a matter of self-respect,' he says. 'The case was Union of India versus Kaushal Kishore Mishra, not a small thing. Once the case was dismissed, I gave up because I had no resources to challenge the order. As it is, it was difficult to make both ends meet. I was doing odd jobs to keep the kitchen fire burning.

'Once I realised I was not going to get my job back as an announcer, I started sitting at the booth because I wanted to put my voice to good use. I don't get paid for this job, even though I put in eight to ten hours every day. I do it out of passion. My biggest reward is that people appreciate what I am doing—they often call me the voice of Kashi.

'Life has been unfair to me, but I don't carry any bitterness. Today I have nothing to complain about. I keep getting voiceover assignments from time to time and whatever little I earn is sufficient to sustain myself and my wife. I have two daughters. They are both well placed. I was able to marry them off without paying a single paisa as dowry, what more can I ask for?

'I see the hand of Lord Vishwanath in placing me there,'—he points to the police booth—'he has ensured that I am at his service.'

I instinctively walk to Dashashwamedha. Priests are hurrying along with their clients before they are all elbowed out by the crowd that would soon gather to watch the Ganga Aarti. Boatmen are urging tourists to watch the aarti from the river. Naga sadhus camping at this ghat have assumed the lotus position; each has a broom made of peacock feathers handy. They are tapping the heads of those making a donation with the broom—imparting a blessing. The day is coming to an end for the pilgrim, the show is about to begin for the tourist.

I am neither a pilgrim nor a tourist, and I have neither the patience nor desire to watch five men waving lamps at the river. I find this exercise as meaningless as the martial ritual that takes place at the Wagah border with Pakistan every sunset. But who am I to say this, when there are hundreds of thousands of people who plan their lives around these events? I decide to walk to Shree Café to say hello—and goodbye—to Santosh Pandey, its owner.

Pandey, freshly bathed and elegantly dressed in a kurta, is sitting at the counter as usual. He has no customers at the moment but soon they will start trickling in.

'I will step out for a bit if you don't mind,' he tells me. 'You can have some coffee in the meantime. On second thought, why don't you come along?'

'Where to?'

'I will treat you to some thandai.'

Thandai means a coolant and the word now figures even in the Oxford Dictionary of English: 'A sweet Indian drink made from a milk base with ingredients such as almonds, saffron, and poppy seeds, traditionally served during the festival of Holi.'

That way, every day is Holi in Banaras. The thandai is as integral to the life of a prototypical Banarasi as tea. Only, his thandai also has a small dose of bhang.

Pandey leads me to Vishwanath Gali and soon our knees are touching a cot that serves as the thandai-seller's stall. The man tells me that he has been in the business for forty years and his family has stalls all over Banaras.

'I open at four in the afternoon and close at eleven, when the temple closes,' he says. 'Even though there is no fixed time to have bhang, people in Banaras usually have it in the evening.'

I learn that there are many ways to imbibe bhang, Shiva's favoured intoxicant. You can make a paste of the leaves and put it in the thandai. You can make small balls of the paste and put it in your mouth before drinking the thandai. You can put the tiny ball in your mouth and swallow it with water. Or you can simply chew on the ball. The ball is known as goli, a bigger ball is gola.

The shopkeeper first hands over a goli to Pandey, who puts it in his mouth. The man then fills two tall glass tumblers with thandai and hands them to us.

'Mine doesn't have bhang, I hope?' I ask him.

'None of them contains bhang,' the shopkeeper assures me. 'I don't mix bhang unless I am specifically asked to. My customers usually take bhang in the form of goli.'

The shopkeeper charges us only for the thandai—the goli, it turns out, is always complimentary. 'I've been having a goli every evening ever since I was in high school,' Pandey tells me. 'It keeps you happy and helps you concentrate better on whatever you are doing.'

A young priest—another customer—who has been overhearing us, interrupts: 'Our job requires us to memorise countless mantras. Do you think that's possible without a dose of bhang? Bhang in small doses is very good for physical and mental health.'

'How long does the effect last?' I ask—of no one in particular.

'Three to four hours,' the shopkeeper replies. 'Ideally, one must take a dump immediately after consuming bhang. Once you do that, the heat generated by the bhang leaves the body and after that you experience peace and happiness.'

54.

IT'S 7.30 P.M. on the night of the snow moon. I begin my walk in the direction of Manikarnika.

I am eager to find the temple Jerome mentioned. I'd thought I knew Banaras well enough by then, but had never even heard of such a temple where fire burns so ferociously that one finds it impossible to hang around beyond a point and where the priest dances on one leg.

I feel woozy as I walk. I suspect the thandai I just drank had traces of bhang in it because this kind of a high can be induced only by an intoxicant. Who minds a little bit of light-headedness when the moon is shining so bright that even the opposite bank of the river is visible? If I were the ruler of Banaras I would order a blackout on a night like this. Let the city be just lit up by the glow of the moon and the pyres.

Even the brightest of halogen lamps is unable to pale the moon. Below one such lamp, near Lalita Ghat, a Naga sadhu is performing the dick trick. I don't know who he's performing for, because there is no audience. Perhaps true sadhus don't need an audience. Only three people are hailing the achievement with raised arms—the sadhu who's standing on the stick, the sadhu whose penile strength is being tested, and another sadhu who is watching the act even as he is cooking.

I click pictures and hurry past them—in case they ask me for money—and arrive at Manikarnika. Five pyres are burning. Dubey, the wood-seller, is unable to recognise me. But his assistant, Kailash—at whose house meals are often cooked over burning logs from pyres—places me instantly.

Two things have changed in Kailash's life since I last saw him three years ago. His father is no more, and his house—thanks to the government's beautification plan—is under demolition. But in spite of these two life-changing tragedies, he looks as happy-go-lucky as ever.

'I will go wherever fate takes me,' he laughs. 'Hardships too are a blessing from Shiva.'

Kailash isn't a sadhu who tests the strength of his dick by making another sadhu stand on it; he is a true Banarasi who has the world placed on his dick. If only I could be like him.

'Is there a temple around here where fire burns all the time and where the priest dances on one leg?' I ask him.

'Do you mean the Masaan temple?'

'I am not sure of its name.'

'I think you mean the Masaan temple—right there!' he points to the old building on whose terrace my mother had been cremated. The terrace has now been given—as part of 'development'—a roof that has chimneys looking like spikes.

'Did we really need those ugly chimneys,' says Kailash. 'The smoke from the pyres never bothered anyone.'

'That's where I cremated my mother,' I point to the far end of the terrace.

'She must have died during the monsoon, did she?'

'Yes, late August.'

'That's when bodies are burnt on the terrace because the ghat gets flooded.'

I walk past the burning pyres—once again I notice a bull sagaciously watching over the cremations—and stand by the building. It abuts the ancient staircase on which funeral processions descend from the galis to the ghat. The base of the building serves as the temple I am looking for. A new bilingual signboard explains why its existence had been hitherto unknown to me:

Shri Baba Masaan Nath Temple
This temple became visible and now available for your visit and darshan after the removal of residential/commercial structures of property no. 6583.
We seek your blessings.

Masaan is a widely-accepted distortion of shamsaan, or burning ghat. Masaan Nath would, therefore, mean the lord of the cremation ground: Shiva. As soon as I step in I am struck by the heat. A pile of wood is burning on a tiled platform built right at the entrance. This is February, the air still chilly, but this place is a furnace.

'Please step aside,' I hear a voice telling me. It's a young man bringing a smouldering log—he is using a pair of rods as forceps—to place it on the burning pile. He retreats and brings another log. He is bringing the logs from the burning pyres. Soon the pile grows tall enough to burn for the rest of the night.

I walk past the furnace into the temple. There is no one else at the moment other than the priest, a wiry, bearded man wearing just a thin saffron dhoti. He is bent over a Shiva lingam, scrubbing it clean.

I have an inherent liking for lean priests. As the middlemen between God and devotees, they come across as more sincere than the ones who look well-fed.

'Have you come for the aarti?' he asks me.

'Yes.'

'Please take a mat and sit down, we will start soon.'

I pick one of the many rolled up mats resting against the wall. Doing so I notice six gigantic damrus—Shiva's hourglass-shaped percussion instrument—hanging on the wall. Shiva's damru fits into his palm, and even the damru you find in shops fits into the palm of an adult, but to grip a damru so large one must be ten times taller and broader. I suspect they are ornamental.

I sit down cross-legged and watch the priest at work. I can not only hear the crackle of the pyres burning right outside but also see the glow of the flames from the windows of the temple. The sanctum sanctorum is built at a level lower than the rest of the temple, with the lingam placed under a granite canopy. The priest, after having scrubbed the lingam and rubbed it with ghee, is now painstakingly building a crown of flowers. He is still adding to the height of the crown when devotees begin to troop in.

One Western woman spreads her mat next to mine. She immediately assumes the lotus position, her spine straight and eyes shut. Two Indian men walk in, each carrying a bottle of Royal Stag whisky. They place the bottles next to the lingam and sit behind me. They are followed by a small group, also from the West: two men and two women, all attired like Indians. By the time the priest is done with the decorations and has lit the lamps, the temple is filled with people, more foreigners than Indians.

And then, just as the priest gets ready to wave a lamp at God, six of the devotees present—one of them a curly-haired white woman—pluck the damrus from the wall. Each of them grips the waist of the damru like one would grip a steering wheel and begins to shake it with great speed, clockwise and anticlockwise, to generate sound. The collective sound of the six gigantic damrus makes me feel like I am inside a washing machine.

This is a rattle that would make you want to leave right away, but once you make peace with it, you are likely to experience a strange kind of peace—or is it a trance? The eyes of the woman next to me are still shut and now her lips have curved into a Mona Lisa smile.

This is a sensation I have never known before: bodies burning outside, wood from the pyres burning inside, the bottles of whisky placed near the lingam, the ear-shattering rattle of the damrus, the bells clanging, and yet the calm on the faces of devotees. At the Vishwanath Temple, the lingam of Shiva is worshipped, but it is here that his spirit is felt—with such great force.

The damru players are sweating. The priest, who has been waving a lamp at the lingam, now does so standing on one leg. He is bathed in sweat as well. Then, still standing on one leg, he hops all the way to the platform on which the pile of wood is burning. Someone switches off the electric lights and the priest, continuing to stand on one leg, waves the lamp at the fire. He's probably worshipping death, the mightiest of forces, whose grip spares none.

The moment the rattle of the damrus stops, silence sweeps through the temple like a cyclone and I feel afloat. Then the chanting begins. The voices are raw and honest, the intonations intense enough to pierce your heart. Once it's all over, the whisky bottles are opened and small portions poured into clay cups for those eager to have a small dose of the Shiva-blessed alcohol. I haven't touched a drink in two years but I find myself extending my hand.

I gulp down my share in one go and find it going straight to my head.

Before leaving, I make a small donation to the priest, who then takes a fistful of ash from the burning pile of wood and rubs it forcefully on my forehead. It's the collective ash from several pyres at Manikarnika, the mother of all cremation grounds. I step out of the temple into the cool February night, the night of the snow moon, feeling a bit like Shiva.

Epilogue: Being Banaras

THE MONSOON SHOULD have drenched Banaras by now but the sky is bland and the air suffocating. It is my shirt that is drenched as I stand at Darbhanga Ghat at eleven o'clock on a Sunday morning, having just arrived from the airport. The Ganga, green and still, has shrunk. The receded waters have exposed the strip of the riverbed hugging the ghats, making them look unkempt.

Why have I chosen to come back at this horrible time of the year? For that matter, why have I chosen to come back this soon, considering my book is done and I should have ideally sent off the manuscript and headed to a cooler place? That's because I was finding it difficult to let go of Banaras.

I walk all the way to Assi—an act of madness, in this heat—and, from time to time, a thought keeps recurring: what if I drop dead in one of the ghats? My soul, of course, will go to heaven, but what will happen to the completed manuscript lying curled up inside my laptop like an about-to-be-born baby?

But I am not worried. Banaras has taught me not to worry. Death is certain. We are all born with labels that bear an expiry date. Only that we never get to look at the label. If that date for me is not today, I'll make it to Assi.

Banaras has taught me many other things as well. A living being is Shiva and so is a dead body. The beautiful is Shiva and so is the ugly. Virtues are Shiva and so are flaws. A stroke of good fortune is Shiva and so is a rough patch. And in the end, no matter who we are, we are just a heap of ash. The simplest of things are most difficult to follow, but at least I have a manual to turn to when required. There is now a bit of Banaras in me.

Assi Ghat looks just the way I had left it a few months ago, sprinkled with young lovers, obstinate bulls and wandering sadhus. But unlike them, I find it too hot to linger. I walk to the neighbourhood of Assi to find some form of rickshaw to take me back to the hotel. These days there are three kinds of rickshaws plying the road running parallel to the river: cycle-rickshaws, autorickshaws and battery-run rickshaws. On second thought, I decide to walk into Pappu's teashop.

To my utter surprise, I find it almost packed, even on a scorching day like this. People occupying its benches are not jobless hangers-on, but men in their fifties or sixties who look important enough to be contributing to society in some way. They come to the shop out of habit: their day isn't complete without a dose of intellectual intercourse at Pappu's shop, the only place outside their home that lets them have their say and feel important.

Right now the men are discussing the pros and cons of living in Banaras. The man doing most of the talking thinks Delhi, Noida and Lucknow are better places to live: life in those places is more organised, roads are wider, and there are far more amenities for the common man than in good old Banaras. I want to tell him that he won't find Pappu's shop in those places, but I don't have the energy to be a part of this think-tank. It is a think-tank that thinks nothing of using the two popular cusswords: *bhosrikay* and *chutiya*. They both more or less mean the same thing—related to the vagina—but *chutiya* is the more benign of the two and is generally used to denote an idiot.

Presently, a middle-aged man walks in and is cheerfully greeted by all. Once he takes off his sunglasses and takes a seat, the conversation switches to Prime Minister Narendra Modi, who, barely weeks ago, had steamrolled the entire Opposition in the general elections to retain his job for another five years.

Modi, because he once again chose to contest from Banaras, is now a poster boy of the city after two successive victories. Most Banarasis believe that India's reins are in competent hands. For them, Modi can do no wrong. Though there are also Banarasis who beg to differ. Like the man who has just walked in.

He declares: 'India is a land of *chutiya*s, that's why Modi won. I would have liked to use the word *moorkh* (foolish), but *chutiya* is more appropriate.'

The man who has been holding forth all this while retorts, 'Do you mean to say even I am a *chutiya* and my wife is also a *chutiya*?'

A third man butts in: 'You say India is a country of *chutiya*s. Therefore, you too count as a *chutiya*, and so does your wife. Don't you?'

The man who had made the sweeping statement caves in. 'Let me amend what I said,' he says. 'I would say the majority of people in India are *chutiya*s.'

The exchange drags on, but it is by no means angry or malicious. The tiny sitting area resonates with laughter even as those pro-Modi and anti-Modi clash. This is democracy, Banaras style, with Pappu's shop serving as the parliament.

All these eighty years, the shop hadn't felt the need to announce its presence to Banarasis. It has been an institution by itself even without a signboard. But now a banner hangs outside, an example of excessive self-praise: 'The world-famous teashop that decides the course of Indian politics and is visited by musicians, professors, vice-chancellors, journalists and politicians seeking intellectual nourishment.'

The banner, apparently hung for the benefit of tourists who are newly interested in Banaras because of Modi, is the only addition I notice at Assi. I am not sure if I like it, but my opinion doesn't matter. I repair to the freezing climes of my hotel room, where the air-conditioner is permanently set at 18 degrees Celsius.

In the evening I find something else that is new: a swanky help centre for those wanting to visit the Vishwanath Temple. It is conveniently close to my hotel at Godowlia and is run by young and smartly-attired attendants, most of them women barely out of their teens. It has a cafeteria, a souvenir shop, lockers and a counter at which tickets to the various daily rituals are sold. You can also buy a ticket for a simple glimpse of Lord Vishwanath: on payment of 300 rupees, a Brahmin will lead you straight to the sanctum sanctorum, bypassing the long queue.

I buy a ticket to the Mangala aarti, the first ritual of the day that begins at three in the morning. The price has now gone up slightly, to 350 rupees. With the ticket in my pocket, I wander to Dashashwamedha, where I am greeted by a sight that's at once horrifying and disappointing. The ghat is occupied by white plastic chairs, a few hundred of them, all facing the river. They are meant to seat those watching the Ganga Aarti, which will begin shortly.

As it is, I was never a great fan of this ritual—there are far more ways of showing respect to the Ganga than by waving lamps—and now I detest it. By sitting on the steps of the ghat to watch the aarti, the tourists adjusted to Banaras, but by providing them with chairs, Banaras is adjusting to tourists. Tomorrow, someone may come up with the idea of a permanent seating arrangement, just like they have done at Wagah, and that would mean the death of Dashashwamedha.

At this hour, Dashashwamedha and its neighbouring ghats are teeming with people, perhaps a few thousand, among them hundreds of skull caps and burqas. Never before have I seen Muslims in such large numbers on the ghats. Their presence lends the dusk a secular touch.

'Why are there so many people here today,' I ask the tea-seller at Darbhanga Ghat.

'Today is a Sunday,' he reminds me. 'Moreover, summer vacations are on. And don't forget, today has been a very hot day; they have come to get some fresh air.'

A boatman steps forward to ask me if I want a ride. I recognise him instantly, but he, quite understandably, doesn't remember ferrying me to Assi a couple of times before. When I tell him that I have travelled in his boat before, he pretends to remember those rides.

'Where would you like to go today,' he asks me.

Since I have nowhere particular to go, I tell him to

take me to Assi. Imagine going to Assi again in a span of a few hours. But that was noon, this is dusk.

From the boat I notice that many other ghats have started their own aarti. Even at Harishchandra Ghat, where three pyres are burning, two men, standing on wooden cots, are waving lamps at the river.

'Why should Harishchandra Ghat have an aarti?' I ask the boatman.

'If other ghats can,' he replies, 'why not Harishchandra Ghat?'

Fair enough. But I suspect the entire exercise is for tourists: when they take a boat ride at dusk, say, five years from now, they will find the entire riverfront dotted with young men moving tiny pieces of fire in circles. How a place can change so quickly.

Assi Ghat is jam-packed. An elaborate aarti is going on here too. The practice here has been going on for a few years now, but it doesn't draw the kind of crowds that Dashashwamedha does. The crowd here, at this hour, is mostly made up of people who have come on an outing. The passage leading from the ghat to the main road is clogged with motorcycles of those headed home after their dose of Assi—barely any place to walk. I squeeze myself through them and, with some difficulty, find a battery-run rickshaw to take me back to Godowlia.

I step into the hotel feeling battered—I would have got here faster had I walked—and fall asleep without having dinner. I wake up in the middle of the night feeling cold. I reach for my phone to look at the time. It's 3.50. I have missed the Mangala aarti.

Around five in the evening daily, the metal barricades guarding the lingam at Vishwanath Temple are removed temporarily so that devotees can get to touch it. At seven o'clock, the evening aarti—called the Saptarshi aarti—begins, and on its completion the barricades are placed again.

'I suggest you buy a ticket for the seven o'clock aarti and reach there by half past six,' the young lady at the ticket counter tells me when I show up at the help centre again. 'If you are lucky, you will get to touch (the lingam) before the aarti begins.'

I do as advised. Sharp at 6.30, armed with the ticket, I arrive at gate no. 4 of the temple. By way of a security check, a constable feels the front pockets of my trousers with his palms and waves me in.

Once inside the temple I realise I am not the only ticket-holder to have arrived before time. There are dozens of others, most of them either Tamils or Telugus. We are berated, from time to time, by the temple staff for crowding the area outside the sanctum sanctorum. We are also being approached by the temple priests—distinguished-looking men in white dhotis, the loose end of the dhoti thrown across their bare torso—looking to make some money.

'The money you paid for the ticket goes to the government,' a priest with an impressive tattoo depicting Shiva on his upper arm tells me, 'but if you make some donation to me, I will make sure you sit right in front when the aarti happens.'

'How much will I have to pay you?'

'Not much, just 500 rupees.'

The ticket for this aarti cost me 180 rupees only—why on earth should I shell out another 500 to a priest who already looks immensely prosperous.

Aimless in Banaras | 251 |

'Let me give it some thought,' I tell him and move away. From one of the doors of the sanctum sanctorum I can see devotees streaming in. They must have been standing in the queue for hours. They are now touching the lingam and moving out in an orderly fashion. No stampede-like situation.

This door, which happens to be closest to the lingam, is being guarded by a tall man in dhoti and kurta. When he notices me nosing around, he waves me away. 'Please don't crowd this place,' he tells me politely, 'I can see you have come for the aarti, but kindly wait elsewhere.'

'I was wondering,' I mumble, 'whether I could step in for a moment and touch Shiva.'

'Not possible,' he says, 'can't you see there is a long queue? How can I allow you?'

When I still linger, he places his hand on my shoulder and guides me in. 'Okay, make it quick!' he says.

I feel the lingam with both my palms. I haven't forgotten that today is Monday—Shiva's day—when people across India throng to Shiva temples to pour water on the lingam and offer it flowers. And here I am, at the most Shiva of all Shiva temples, getting to touch Him.

I step out feeling triumphant. I offer the man 500 rupees but he refuses it and waves me away. Since I find it pointless now to wait for the aarti, I decide to leave. As I walk out, I wonder if that man could have been Shiva himself. Since this is Banaras, I am entitled to such imagination.

This book opens with a scene from 2009—my mother's cremation at Manikarnika, which inspired the book in the first place—whereas these final lines are being written in 2019. I hadn't, of course, intended to time it that way, but its completion happens to mark her tenth death anniversary. As if destiny had decided to extract a timely tribute from me. I feel almost like that son who built a temple at Manikarnika in his mother's honour to compensate for her motherly duties. So what if the temple earned the mother's curse and began to lean, it remains a defining feature of the riverfront. Without it, Banaras wouldn't be Banaras.

Acknowledgements

The prologue first appeared in a 2016 *Lonely Planet* travel anthology, *True Stories from the World's Best Writers*, under the title, *A Cremation in Banaras*.

A few of the encounters described in the book were originally recounted, in much shorter form, in pieces I wrote for *The Hindu*.

Heartfelt thanks are due to my editor Prita Maitra, for tidying up the manuscript, and Gautam Padmanabhan, the CEO of Westland, who has been consistent in his support for my works.

www.ingramcontent.com/pod-product-compliance
Lightning Source LLC
LaVergne TN
LVHW010313070526
838199LV00065B/5549